Animal Clinic
for
Cats

Other similar titles from Random House Value Publishing

Animal Clinic for Dogs

Understanding Your Pet

Psychic Pets

The Personality of the Dog

The Personality of the Cat

The Cat Owner's Manual

Animal Clinic
for
Cats

JIM HUMPHRIES, D.V.M.

GRAMERCY BOOKS
New York

Copyright © 1994 by St. Francis Productions, Inc.

This 1998 edition is published by Gramercy Books, an imprint of Random House Value Publishing, Inc., by arrangement with Howell Book House, A Prentice Hall Macmillan Company, 15 Columbus Circle, New York, NY 10023.

Gramercy Books and colophon are trademarks of Random House Value Publishing, Inc.

(Originally published as: *Dr. Jim's Animal Clinic for Cats: What People Want to Know*)

Printed in the United States of America

Library of Congress Cataloging–in–Publication Data

Humphries, Jim.
    [Dr. Jim's animal clinic for cats]
    Animal clinic for cats / Jim Humphries.
       p. cm.
    Originally published : Dr. Jim's animal clinic for cats. New York :
Howell Book House, c1994.
    Includes index.
    ISBN 0–517–18905–4
    1. Cats—Miscellanea. 2. Cats—Health—Miscellanea. 3. Cats—
Diseases—Miscellanea. I. Title.
    [SF447.H94 1998]
    636.8'03—dc21   97–29143
                                            CIP

Random House Value Publishing, Inc.
New York • London • Toronto • Sydney • Auckland
http://www.randomhouse.com/

Animal Clinic for Cats

9 8 7 6 5 4 3 2 1

Contents

Acknowledgments

My career in both veterinary medicine and in the electronic media has been affected by many people. They all deserve a gracious thank you for their teachings, support, encouragement and belief in what I do. My fondest memories are of those people who saw into the future and knew that my sacrifices and crazy ideas would eventually gain recognition. Blazing a trail can be a scary venture, but the fear was eased, and good advice and direction were given by these true friends.

First I would like to thank my wife, Pat. A true animal lover, Pat has always impressed me with her compassion and caring for any kind of creature. Even though what I do is way out of her comfort zone, she has constantly supported my ventures since our meeting six years ago. Her most valuable contribution is keeping my feet firmly planted on the ground and helping me keep an eye on the real goal. She persuaded me to stop trying to steer the ship so forcefully and let God's universal plan take its course. As soon as I did, things began to happen. Pat is also responsible for much of the writing, proofing and editing of my works in both print and the electronic media. She has a natural knack for taking a complex subject and making it easy to read, hear or see on video. She is the most natural animal trainer I have ever seen as is evidenced by our five great pets, and her National Top Ten Arabian mare. The relationship I have with Pat is the accomplishment in life of which I am most proud.

My mother clearly had the most early effect on my life and on my becoming a veterinarian. Her early teachings about compassion and respect for life, along with her encouraging my medical curiosity, lit the fire that still burns for this passion I have. To this day she never stops encouraging me and gets more pure joy out of my accomplishments than anyone. I'll never be able to repay her for all she has done. She'll probably never get tired of hearing me say, *Thanks, Mom*.

Dr. James Merle Baker was like a father to me. He taught me fundamental principles of veterinary medicine, client relations, animal care and compassion. Truly my best memories as a young adult were riding with Doc on calls, looking up complicated diseases and making textbook information apply to the real world. Doc made learning fun and practical. His kindness and encouragement were instrumental in my making it through the rigors of veterinary school. He is a true hero and a savior to countless thousands of animals in south Texas.

Next, because this book is based on my years as a talk radio show host, I must thank the man who gave me that initial break—Dan Bennett. He taught me radio formatics, the importance of hitting commercial breaks and keeping the show moving with high energy. His criticism always made the show better and today my show is both informative and entertaining because Dan taught me how to mix the two.

Dale Brandon is my media and public relations consultant—but more than that he is a true friend. He has taken the foundation and framework I've built over the past eight years and turned it into a truly multi-media operation that reaches hundreds of thousands of pet owners. Dale gets real joy from my success. Dale's belief in me and his incredible enthusiasm was the exact prescription this doctor needed to continue on into uncharted territory.

Several other very important people believed in me when self-doubt loomed. Betty White is a major television star and animal lover. Heaven knows, she is approached by thousands of people and organizations every year for endorsements and to make demands on her time. Yet from the beginning, Betty has agreed to be a guest on my radio and television shows and has encouraged me every step of the way. That meant a great deal and kept me going when it was tough. Thanks Betty! . . . and thanks to Gail Clark, her personal secretary.

From a business standpoint, Roger Winter is my mentor. Roger is a highly successful businessman and keeps common sense and fairness his top priority. Roger has given me valuable advice for years and never expected anything in return. His creativity and savvy help guide me through some difficult business decisions. Roger takes great pride in seeing other people succeed and I am lucky to call him my friend.

Dr. Karen Fling and Dr. David Goodnight are two colleagues who have always supported my media career when others scoffed at my attempts to reach the public. They have never flinched in their support of my public education efforts and help me stay current in an ever-advancing field. This is noteworthy because many of my colleagues have tried to make this difficult path even more so, but these two doctors are not only excellent veterinarians, they also know what's best for the profession.

Finally, I thank everyone at Howell Book House. Sean Frawley and Madelyn Larsen are top professionals and their input on this work was invaluable. They have been there every step of the way on every project and I would not have been able to keep up the pace without their positive expectancy. They know the true value of pets in our lives and were eager to help me with my first two works! Thank you for making these dreams a reality.

And thank you, Father, for the dramatic display of power once I finally shed the yoke and let the universal auto pilot take back control.

Foreword

Have you ever picked up a dictionary with the intention of looking up one word and found it difficult not to linger and read on? The same thing applies to *Dr. Jim's Animal Clinic for Cats* and its equally fine companion piece, *Dr. Jim's Animal Clinic for Dogs*. The question-and-response format keeps leading you on and becomes like a conversation about one of our favorite subjects. However, in the event that a concise answer to a specific problem is needed in a hurry, it is directly accessible, not buried in more extraneous information than is needed at that moment.

It is also reassuring to find some of your own inquiries right there on the printed page. So yours wasn't such a dumb question after all, was it? As a result, the next time you take your friend to the veterinarian, hopefully, you will feel encouraged to ask him or her for information, as well as simply listing symptoms. Even a busy animal doctor welcomes your interest, and it will establish a comfortable dialogue between you that can only be beneficial to your pet's future visits.

Although Dr. Humphries' answers are crisp and to the point, there is an underlying warmth throughout that reveals how much he genuinely cares about his animal subjects.

This is a book to keep within reach.

BETTY WHITE

Introduction

I have always loved animals. I am constantly amazed when I hear people say they don't like animals, because for me it has always been such a natural thing. My mother was allergic to cats, so as a child I never had the chance to be exposed to cats. However, working in our hometown veterinary clinic after school, I quickly became fascinated with cats.

I was lucky to become a friend of the "clinic cat" Roger. This cat never met a person he didn't like. He was the best goodwill and PR ambassador we could have. I soon learned that cats have unique personalities and that they rely on their actions, rather than their appearance, to demonstrate their special personality. Dogs, on the other hand, are judged much more by their outward appearance: big dog, little dog, happy dog, sad dog, cute dog, ugly dog. Before you even touch a dog, you have formed an opinion of how he'll be by his appearance.

Working with cats in a clinical setting taught me how different their medical problems and peculiarities were. In delivering their care, a person must adopt a whole new attitude. You should not force a cat to accept a needle, for example. Being too forceful, even with good intentions, can be fatal to a very sick cat.

Dr. J. M. Baker was our hometown veterinarian for many years. Doc was a kind man who worked harder than anyone I had ever seen. He went out of his way to accommodate my great interest in veterinary medicine. More than anyone, Dr. Baker is why I became a veterinarian. He could handle the biggest bull, the smartest horse and the sickest cat with firm, kind attention. Much of what I learned from Dr. Baker stays with me today.

I love both large and small animals. Each group has its own unique set of problems, cures and environmental settings in which to work. However, small animal medicine is special to me because I am able to spend more time with each case and it offers more opportunity for me to use my knowledge of internal medicine and diagnostics. It affords me the opportunity to practice advanced and detailed surgeries, as well as study animal behavior.

I practiced for about six years in various settings: government work, medical center practice, emergency clinic specialty and private practice. After moving to Dallas, I became involved with the local humane society. Here I learned firsthand of some of the terrible situations many animals find themselves in. It seemed strange that I had never come across these issues. They certainly were not discussed in veterinary school. I became more sensitive to overpopulation, animal abuse and neglect.

In addition to humane issues, I became fascinated by the subject of human and animal interactions. I read books and articles and learned about the tremendous, almost miraculous, benefits of animals' interactions with cancer patients, recovering heart attack patients, the elderly, autistic and handicapped children, prisoners and head-injured people.

I began a mobile veterinary practice partly to serve these people and found those years to be very rewarding. I became very close to many of my clients—closer than one ever gets by seeing them in the sterile environment of an animal hospital. I was visiting their homes and they felt like I was a true friend.

Because of the unique nature of my practice I was asked to be a guest on a local radio program on KLIF, a newly formed all-talk station in Dallas–Ft. Worth. After two appearances, the program director, Dan Bennett, called me into his office and asked me if I'd like my own show! Of course I jumped at the opportunity. The thousands of times I had gone over the flea control message or told the heartworm disease story to one person at a time in the clinic raced through my mind. I thought of the hundreds of hours I had spent with people in their homes going over pet care items. Now, when I told these things, thousands of people would hear and benefit. I was ready.

A large pet-products manufacturer based in Dallas convinced me to try to take the radio talk show to a national network. Eventually I was able to line up just the minimum amount of sponsorships needed to pay for the very expensive satellite linkup time, and my show went on the air in 35 cities as "Dr. Jim's Animal Clinic."

Today my show is heard every Saturday afternoon in almost 100 cities and I have answered over 35,000 calls on talk radio. I have developed the talent for sizing up a question very quickly and delivering a highly focused and concise answer, *and that is the basis for this book*.

I feel I know better than anyone what people want to know about their pets. I have invested years of study and research into developing the proper answers for medical, surgical, behavioral and training topics.

In this book I answer many questions that are consistently asked week after week. In Part I, Common Questions, you will learn the right way to choose a kitten or cat, *and* a veterinarian to care for it. We love to travel with our pets, and cats have special travel needs. You'll learn how to deal with them here. I am a strong advocate of adopting pets from a humane society or an animal shelter. In the spring and summer these places are overrun with kittens that need a loving home, therefore I cover key points in properly adopting a cat. And as you can imagine, I do not believe people should breed their pets, so I have included many of the questions people ask about birth control and reproduction. Having lost many beloved pets due to old age or disease, and having gone through the flood of deep emotions many times, Chapter 6 discusses how to help old cats, along with the ways to handle the loss of your pet friend.

Part II is very important. It covers home-care grooming tips. Now you should be able to bathe your cats at home and keep them smelling good, looking good and more fun to be with. Many of the products discussed have a direct bearing on your cat's health and, when used properly, will save you hundreds of dollars in grooming and veterinary bills. All the behavioral issues associated with domesticated cats are covered in Part III. These topics generate the most calls on the show. From introducing cats into a new household, to proven ways to retrain your cat to use its litter box, this section is packed with real-world, common sense advice that will help you and your cats enjoy each other more. Even though this is not surgery or breakthrough medicine, it may be just as life saving for a cat that scratches the furniture or bites your spouse!

Everyone is concerned with controlling fleas and ticks, worms and mites. Flea-bite dermatitis is the number one complaint in veterinary offices for both dogs and cats. New technology is released every day, and a great deal of bad information gets passed along as well. Toxoplasmosis is a serious concern for cat owners and tapeworms are a universal problem so you need solid advice on the control of these parasites and you'll find it in Part IV.

The pet food business has changed completely in the last ten years. With hundreds of new brands, some claiming they are not only the best, but also that all the others are bad for your cat, it is very confusing! Part V attempts to bring some sanity back to the issue of pet nutrition and explains how to choose a pet food that will be good for your cat and not break your budget.

As a veterinarian, I am most interested in true medicine and surgery for pet animals. Part VI covers the most common medical questions people have asked me. From vaccinations to cancer, from heart disease to heat stroke you will get the same easy-to-understand advice, which will steer you in the right direction with your own veterinarian. Also, itching and scratching pets are so common that not a radio show goes by without someone asking my first, second or third opinion on how to help their cat. I have offered up the best information available today to deal with this maddening problem. Cats have unique skin diseases and need unique cures; you'll find answers to many of the questions about them, as well.

Finally, every time it is Saturday and the moon is full, I get the weirdest and funniest calls. I thought you would enjoy reading about some of these calls in Part VII, in the chapter called Full-Moon Saturdays.

Just a word about my philosophy. I hate wishy-washy advice. Far too many talk show hosts, especially in how-to fields, are under the impression they cannot be specific. They are afraid to step on someone's toes, or mention a brand name, or be too specific because someone will come along and point a finger saying they were wrong. Many times it is easier to be general and vague and not make waves. But in my opinion, *that is not helpful.*

When you are in a dark room you want to know where the light switch is, not a lecture on light-emitting particles. You want to know what is the best switch, the name, the color, the shape, where to get it and how much it costs. You don't care that there are some forty switches at your hardware retailer and you don't want to hear, "Ask your friendly sales associate which one's best for you." That's why people call a talk show with an expert host!

Therefore I am proud of my concise, to-the-point, helpful, how-to answers. I am happy that my listeners get "golden nuggets" of advice on everything from cats that mark the stereo speakers, to when it's time to say good-bye to a beloved family pet. I don't worry about what some company or manufacturer might say about my comments concerning their product. My only concern during a talk show is that I give the best advice I can muster at that moment.

No doubt there are doctors and animal behaviorists who know more about a specific subject than I do. But this book is not about details, or about the Nth degree, *it's about helpful golden nuggets of information.*

Dr. Jim's Animal Clinic for Cats and the companion volume, *Dr. Jim's Animal Clinic for Dogs*, are compilations of the most frequently asked questions on talk radio and my very focused, easy-to-implement solutions. I've organized the information in such a way that you can access it without having to read the whole book. All of the quotations at the beginning of each chapter are actual talk-radio calls—*they're not made up!* All of the questions in each chapter are actual talk radio callers' questions.

Not every category could be covered in this book but eventually will be with subsequent editions. I hope my years of experience and proven techniques are helpful to you and your cats. I know how much pets have meant to me personally, and I have seen firsthand how important they are to thousands of singles, young couples, parents, children and seniors. It is my greatest wish that you and your family will enjoy the relationship with your pets more because of this book. Enjoy.

"Now let's go to the next caller. . . . Hi, you're on the air with Dr. Jim. . . ."

This book is not intended as a substitute for the medical advice of your veterinarian. The reader should regularly consult a veterinarian in matters relating to his or her cat's health and particularly in respect to any symptoms that may require diagnosis or medical attention.

PART I

COMMON QUESTIONS

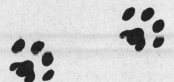

CHAPTER 1

Choosing a Cat and Choosing a Veterinarian

"Dr. Jim, I think there is a book that all cats read, called 'How To Pick a Person.'"

"Oh really? Why's that?"

"Every stray cat or kitten in the city seems to know to come right to our back door. They know right away that my wife is a pushover, but hard as I try not to get attached, everyone of them knows just what to do to sneak into my heart."

Cats are wonderful pets. As a matter of fact, cats have now surpassed dogs as the most popular pets in America! Veteran cat owners know the affection, entertainment and companionship that pet cats offer. Cats are also fastidiously clean, do well in any size home and require less care than a dog. I've often said that anyone who doesn't like cats just hasn't met the right cat yet. In fact, some of the "cat craziest" clients I've had were former "dog people" with little use for cats until they were adopted by the right stray.

Contrary to what many people think, cats are not aloof, totally independent creatures with little desire for interaction with their owners. (Ask any owner of a Siamese.) Some breed types are more demanding of attention than others, but any breed (or mixed breed) that is raised correctly and well socialized will make a wonderful companion.

Once you've chosen your cat, you'll need to choose a veterinarian. The relationship between you and your veterinarian is extremely important. You will trust this person with the life of one of your best friends, one who often cannot tell you if he is hurt, or where.

Besides a professional-looking clinic that is clean, well lit and odor free, I feel the most important criterion is a veterinarian who stays up-to-date with the latest advances in animal medicine. Veterinary medical information doubles every six to seven years. This means veterinarians must continue to study by attending continuing-education seminars and by reading professional journals, or in a few years they will know only half of what they should.

It takes real commitment for a busy doctor to keep current. Ask your veterinarian if he or she regularly attends continuing education courses, or look to see if the doctor displays continuing education certificates on his walls. Check to see if the hospital is certified by the American Animal Hospital Association (AAHA), as they certify only the best.

Q: *My twelve-year-old daughter has always wanted a cat, and I've agreed to get her one for her birthday next month. I don't really know much about cats. I know there's a big difference in size and personality among breeds of dogs, but what about cats?*

A: Obviously cats don't vary much in size. In fact, among the recognized registered breeds there is only about ten pounds difference between the largest breed, the Ragdoll, and the smallest breed, the Singapura. Most breeds of cats are about the same size, and all of them will fit into any living arrangement. Cats adapt well to living in any size home, in rural, suburban or urban settings.

There are some personality differences to the different breed types. Basically, the more svelte, long, slender-body-type cats with narrow, triangular heads have more Siamese-type personality traits. These cats tend to be very outgoing, more vocal and need lots of attention from their owners. In fact, they demand it. They have a high energy level, love to play and tend to stay very kittenlike.

On the opposite end of the spectrum are the shorter, rounder body-type cats with round heads and smaller ears.

These cats have more Persian-type personality traits. These cats are very easygoing, rarely vocal and more laid back. They are affectionate, but will not be all over you for attention all the time. They have low energy levels and are more reserved.

Cats whose body types and head shapes fall in between these two extremes, usually have personalities that also fall in between the active, demanding Siamese-type and the quiet, reserved Persian-type. These cats have moderate energy levels, moderate need for attention and tend to be only moderately vocal.

So, depending on whether your daughter would like a constant feline companion who will want lots of play and attention or a more sedate feline friend who will be happy with the occasional petting and attention, she may be happier with one type than another.

Another thing to take into consideration is whether to get a longhaired or shorthaired cat. While all cats require some regular grooming, cats with long and thick coats, such as Persians and Himalayans, need daily grooming to keep their coats in good condition and free of mats. These cats also shed more hair, especially in the spring and fall.

Q: *I'm going to be getting a new kitten soon. How do I make sure she's healthy?*

A: That's a good question. It's heartbreaking to come home with a new kitten only to find out she's sick, perhaps seriously. The best prevention is to try to pick a healthy kitten and then get it to your veterinarian right away for a "new-kitty" checkup.

Your new kitten should be alert and playful. She should have bright, clear eyes with no tearing or discharge. Her nose should be moist and clear of any drainage or discharge. Look in her ears, they should be clean and dry. Dirty or waxy ears can indicate ear mites or infection.

Her coat should be soft and smooth, never rough or patchy. When you run your fingers along her body you shouldn't feel any scabs or rough spots. She shouldn't have any bald spots, which could indicate ringworm.

She should be free of "dirt." Place her on a light-colored surface and brush your hand through her coat a couple of times.

If the surface has dark-colored "dirt specks" on it following this, the kitten has fleas. "Flea dirt" is actually dried blood excrement from the fleas.

Check under her tail for any signs of wetness or staining that might indicate diarrhea.

Most of all, observe her for alertness and playfulness. A kitten who hangs back and doesn't appear curious or playful may not feel well.

The kitten should be at least eight weeks old and should have been examined by a veterinarian and received her first vaccinations. Ask to see the vaccination record from the veterinarian.

After you select a kitten, make sure you have an agreement with the seller that you can return the kitten and receive a full refund of your money within an agreed upon time if she is found by your veterinarian to be ill or have genetic medical problems. Take your kitten to see your veterinarian as soon as possible, preferably by the next day.

Q: *Are there differences in personalities among litter mates?*
A: There can be. When you choose a new kitten, take some time to watch the whole litter play. Instead of immediately going to each kitten and picking it up, observe how they react to your presence. Take a cat toy or some yarn and pull it back and forth in front of you. The kitten who bounds right over to investigate is confident and outgoing. A kitten who takes more encouragement to come to you and play is a little more timid and takes more time to get used to new situations. A kitten who runs and hides is extremely timid. It may have had a bad experience or been mishandled.

If you have an active household, with children or other pets, you should pick a confident, outgoing kitten. If you have a quiet life style and no other pets, you can choose either an outgoing kitten or a more timid one and probably be just fine. I would recommend you stay away from a kitten that runs and hides. It's sometimes tempting to try to rehabilitate these shy cases, but it can be difficult and requires time and patience. Some of these kittens never become very interactive companions.

Q: *My husband and I want to get a companion cat for our two-year-old tabby. Where do suggest looking for a new kitten or cat?*

A: I always suggest people check with their local shelter or humane society for a new kitten or cat. These places are overrun with kittens every spring and summer. Adult cats of every type and age are available at all times. Mixed-breed cats are great companions and have precious few medical problems. Because developing a line of purebred cats involves inbreeding the desired lines, purebred cats tend to have more medical problems and certainly have a greater tendency toward genetically inherited problems than do mixed breeds.

Also, some of the best cat companions I've ever had have been stray cats looking for a home. Just be sure you don't expose such a cat to your established household cats until you have taken the new cat to the doctor's office for a checkup, deworming and vaccinations.

Q: *I have my heart set on a purebred cat, but I'm not sure what breed I want. What do you suggest?*

A: If you are set on a purebred cat, you are probably looking for either a specific "look" or a particular personality type. I suggest you read up on the types of cats you are interested in. There are books available on all the most popular breeds as well as many good books that cover all the recognized breeds in a single book. Call a few breeders or owners, ask some questions about the cat's personality, genetic problems and general maintenance. You can find lists of breeders in the yearbooks published by the Cat Fanciers' Association and the Cat Fanciers' Federation. Breeders often advertise in cat magazines, such as *Cat Fancy*. Many pet shops have bulletin boards where breeders can leave their cards, and there is always the newspaper classifieds.

One of the best places to learn about purebred cats is at a cat show. Remember, breeders will be biased toward their breed, but after looking at twenty or thirty breeds of cats, you should have a better idea of what you want.

Q: *I lost my old cat, Snowball, a couple of months ago. I'd like to get another cat now, but I'm worried about a kitten getting lonely. I'm single and I work during the day. What do you think?*

A: You're right. A kitten would get lonely all by himself all day. Not to mention that kittens, like all baby animals, need a certain degree of supervision. Kittens are very energetic and need someone (either human or animal) to play with in order to help expend all this energy. Kittens also must be taught the rules of living in your home and that does require some time, effort and patience.

You may want to consider adopting an adult cat if you are busy and don't have the time (or patience) for training a new kitten. A young cat of one to five years of age will have plenty of playfulness left without the excess energy of a kitten. Since cats (especially indoor cats) can live into their late teens and twenties, an older cat of ten years or so is often a great new pet that can be with you for many years. These cats are more settled, but still plenty affectionate and interactive. Adult cats often already know the rules of living with humans. If they don't, retraining is not as hard as most people think. It just takes a little effort and patience.

An added bonus is that many of these adult cats are already neutered, spayed or declawed. Just pick a cat that suits your personality and life style. The best way to do this is to spend some quiet time with the cat where you can get to know each other. Many humane societies and shelters have "quiet rooms" where you can take the cat and spend some time getting acquainted.

In fact, if you are gone most of the day, I suggest two cats. This way they can keep each other occupied and entertained during the time you are gone. Single cats in homes where people are gone most of the time can become very bored and lonely, as well as lazy and overweight.

Q: *Our family will be getting a new kitten this weekend. What preparations should we make for her arrival?*

A: Since you know you'll be getting your new kitten this weekend, go ahead and call your veterinarian and make an appointment for a new-kitten checkup. If he can't do it Saturday, then make an appointment for first thing Monday morning.

Find out what type of food the kitten is on currently and get some of the same brand and type. Get a litter box and fill it with two to three inches of litter. Buy food and water bowls, grooming tools, a scratching post, several kitty toys and a plastic travel kennel. Now, you're ready! Make sure you use the travel kennel to transport the kitten home as well as to and from the veterinarian.

When you bring the new little guy home, place him first in his litter box so that he knows exactly where it is. Offer him a little food and water and then leave him alone to explore the room. Don't worry if he runs immediately under the bed and hides. That's normal. After all, he's been taken away from his mom and his brothers and sisters, not to mention the only surroundings he's ever known.

Let him take his time to get used to things. Don't handle him too much and don't let children play with him until he gets used to things (at least a day or two). If you have other pets, let him be in a room with a closed door, away from them. Give him some time to become comfortable with you and his new surroundings before introducing him to your other pets. (See Chapter 11, Introducing a New Pet). He will soon become comfortable and will, no doubt, be into everything you're doing.

Do a safety check for potential hazards. Keep toilet lids down. Tuck electrical cords away. Make sure window screens fit tightly so he doesn't accidentally escape. Be careful about hot burners and irons. Watch out when closing doors on refrigerators, washers and dryers, as well as closets and dresser drawers. Kittens are curious and may slip into any of these places when you're not looking.

Q: *I like my veterinarian, but sometimes I have to wait thirty or forty-five minutes past my appointment time. I don't think that's right. What do you think?*

A: I understand your frustration at having to wait to see the veterinarian, but it could be that your doctor was unexpectedly delayed by an emergency or had to spend more time than expected with another client ahead of you. He may have a very busy practice, which could be a sign that he is highly thought of. If this happens occasionally it's best to be understanding. If you consistently have to wait past your appointment time, talk to your doctor about it. Perhaps he can recommend a different time of day or day of the week when he is typically not as busy. Saturday mornings are typically very busy times at clinics nationwide!

Q: *We really like our vet, but he seems to be gone a lot. The last several times we've gone in we've seen someone new each time. We'd like your opinion on this.*

A: I recommend you talk to your doctor about your concerns. Try to tactfully find out why he is gone so often. If he's gone fishing all those times, then he may not be very committed to his practice and the level of care is sure to reflect that. On the other hand, he may be gone to veterinary continuing-education seminars or could be working toward an advanced degree in surgery or another specialty. This would speak highly of his commitment to staying current on the latest advances in animal medicine.

Talk to your doctor and make it known to him that it is important for you to develop a consistent relationship with one veterinarian. Your doctor may be able to tell you certain days or times when he is always available. You will have to decide for yourself, after speaking with him, if it is a situation you can live with. If not, you may want to consider developing a relationship with the veterinarian who fills in for him, or changing clinics altogether.

Q: *Our doctor sees a lot of cows and horses. When we take our cat to see him, he seems in a hurry to get through with us. I feel our cat doesn't get the same priority or level of care as the large animals do. What would you suggest we do?*

A: This is a common complaint among small pet owners who go to a "mixed-practice" veterinarian, one who sees both large and small animals. Horses and cattle often comprise the bulk of these practices. Usually the veterinarian has to go to these patients rather than them coming to him, so he is often out of the clinic. Add to this the considerable monetary value of some of these equine and bovine patients and you can see why most mixed-practice veterinarians concentrate more on their large patients, than on dogs and cats. It is also difficult enough for a doctor to stay current on medical advances in either large- or small-animal medicine, without trying to stay up-to-date on *both*. All this is not to say that there are not some veterinarians who provide excellent care for both large and small animals. There are. However, if your veterinarian gives the impression that he much prefers cows to cats, then that will probably reflect in his work as well. You, as the client, need to be happy with your veterinarian and feel that he is interested in your cat. You may want to consider changing to a small-animal doctor. In some cases, there is only one veterinarian in a large area and so he must see all animals, small and large. In such a case, talk to your doctor and see if he sets aside special times to see only small animals, such as Saturday mornings.

Q: *We've recently moved to Kansas from Kentucky. How do we find a good veterinarian here?*

A: Start by asking friends, neighbors and co-workers who own cats which veterinarian they go to. Find out how well they like their doctor and why. Then develop a list of these doctors and others that are within your area. Some veterinarians are now specializing in cats. See if you have one of these special hospitals in your area.

Next call each clinic and ask if the doctor specializes in any particular type of pet or problem, what their office hours are and how they handle emergencies after hours. Notice how you are treated by the office staff on the phone. If they seem warm, friendly and helpful on the phone, that's a good sign they will treat you and your cat well in person. If you don't have a good feeling about the clinic from your phone call, eliminate it from your list.

Next, review your notes from your phone calls and note which clinics seem to best fit your particular needs. Pick a clinic whose office hours are convenient to you and which is close enough to your home in case of emergency.

Choose a clinic or two to visit. You might take your kitty in for a routine procedure such as yearly vaccinations for your first visit. On this visit, notice how you are treated by the office staff. They should be friendly and helpful. Notice if the clinic is clean, well lit and odor free. Ask about payment policies, if cash is required at the time of treatment, or if credit cards are accepted.

Notice how the technicians and the veterinarian handle your cat and how they relate to you. Cats require some special handling and special understanding about behavior and restraint. Find a clinic that is sensitive to these special needs. Do pick a veterinarian you feel comfortable talking to, one who takes time to answer all your questions, and one who seems caring and relates well to your cat. If the first clinic doesn't meet your needs, try again.

Q: *When we visit the animal hospital, the technicians seem to do most of the work. We like our doctor, but we'd like to see him once in a while. Is this normal?*

A: No, it's not normal. You need the opportunity for good two-way communication with your veterinarian. You will have some questions you want to ask him and it's important he have the opportunity to examine your cat in your presence so that you can both discuss any concerns. Some very busy doctors have to use technicians more than they would like to, but it's important that you voice your concerns to the staff. Ask to speak to the doctor and make it known to him that you would like him to make an effort to spend more time with you when you bring your cat in. If the situation doesn't improve, you may want to consider finding another veterinarian.

Q: *My family has been going to the same vet for years. When we take our cat in, he never talks to us much, just prescribes pills and moves on. Do you think we should look for a new vet?*

A: Yes. Loyalty is one thing, but to keep going to a veterinarian just because your family has always used him is not a good reason. Since your family has used this doctor for years, I imagine he is probably an older veterinarian and may be burned out on practice and not have an interest in communicating with his clients.

Good communication with your veterinarian is a must. He should explain thoroughly any illness or disease your cat has. He should discuss treatment options with you and explain why he recommends a certain course of treatment. You should be shown any X rays or test results and these should be explained to you. In short, you and your veterinarian should be a team, caring for your cat together. If it doesn't feel like that, you need to find a new doctor.

Q: *Our cat has been diagnosed with leukemia and he has seen our vet many times for his treatment. Now she wants to send him to a specialist at a university. Do you think we should take him?*

A: Yes, this is a good sign that your doctor stays up-to-date on the latest advances in animal medicine, that she communicates with experts and is not afraid to refer difficult cases to the appropriate specialist. Your veterinarian knows that veterinary teaching hospitals have access to the latest technology and equipment. Much of this type of equipment is extremely expensive, far beyond the scope of a private clinic. This is much the same as having your own family doctor refer you to a specialist or to a hospital for advanced treatment.

Q: *Our vet doesn't really seem to like cats. We feel like we should say something to him about this, but we don't know what to say. Any suggestions?*

A: First of all, if you're not comfortable talking to your veterinarian, you need to find a different doctor for that reason alone. It is essential that you feel you can comfortably communicate with him at all times.

There are some veterinarians who like dogs but don't care for cats, or who like large animals but could do without small ones. If your doctor doesn't seem to like cats, I would definitely find a new doctor. A veterinarian's entire job requires him to deal with animals. He should clearly like them. You wouldn't want to take your child to a pediatrician who didn't seem to like children. Your cat is, after all, your friend, someone very important to you. You need to feel confident that his doctor likes him and cares about him.

Q: We really like our vet, but we just went in for yearly shots and a checkup and got a bill for $100! We were shocked. Isn't that too high?

A: That depends on what was done for $100. If your cat received only her yearly vaccinations then that may be too high. If, however, she received an examination, deworming, nutritional counseling and perhaps a prescription diet, you may have gotten quite a bargain.

If you consider what you pay for health care for your pet compared to what you pay for yourself you will find you are getting a great value indeed. Most veterinarians work long hours and do not make a great deal of money. Their focus is on being able to provide good medical care to their patients. Medical costs have increased dramatically in the past years in all areas, veterinary medicine being no different. The good news is there are now a few companies who are beginning to offer medical insurance for pets.

CHAPTER 2

Traveling with Cats

"We've heard you talk about the importance of keeping cats in a carrier when traveling. I called to tell you I know first hand that's true. We were on vacation with some friends in their motor home last year. They were nice enough to let us take Mittens along. About ten miles out Mittens got frightened and started to run frantically around the motor home. At one point she got under Bill's feet while he was driving! When he pushed her out from under his feet she leapt for his head and knocked his hair off. We didn't even know Bill wore a toupee!"

Americans love to travel. They take almost 500 million minivacations of four days or less every year. Cat lovers are faced with a dilemma at these times; do they trust their precious pet to someone else's care or do they take her along.

Cats present a special problem because many don't do well when away from their familiar surroundings. Cats typically like routine and sameness and when that changes, it can cause stress and problems.

There are many cats who love to travel and would be quite hurt if they did not get to go along. For some owners, leaving their precious pet behind in someone else's care is simply not an option. Others are comfortable with pet sitters or kennels. You have to judge your cat individually. Whatever you decide to do when you travel, plan ahead for the comfort and safety of your pet.

Cats can slip out a door very quickly, and if you're hundreds or thousands of miles from home, you may not get them back. Always have kitty in a cat carrier or on a harness type restraint with a leash whenever a door is opened! Of course, I.D. tags are a must along with all the other care items that must accompany a cat.

Q: *I've heard you talk about the importance of using a cat carrier when traveling with a cat. My cat has never been in a carrier before and she wants nothing to do with the new carrier I bought her. Any suggestions?*

A: Don't worry. You know cats don't like anything that's not their idea! You just have to make her think that this whole cat carrier thing is something she wants to do.

First of all, don't force her into the carrier. That's the best way to insure a fight anytime you want to put her in it. Take advantage of her natural curiosity. Leave the carrier out in an area she frequents, like the kitchen or your bedroom. Take the door off and put a piece of your clothing, like an old T-shirt (unwashed) and a new catnip toy inside. Then just leave the carrier there for several days or a week and let her investigate it on her own.

Once the cat seems unbothered by the carrier, move her food bowl into it (with the door still off). Let her go in and out as she pleases. You can call her over to the carrier, but don't carry her over to it and don't physically try to get her to go in. Continue to feed her in the carrier until she goes in and out without a fuss.

At this point, take the food bowl out and put some really tasty, favorite treat into the carrier. Praise your kitty for going in and gently restrain her at the door for just a second or two, then let her out. Do this a couple of times a day for several days, then try it with the door on. Do the same thing, but this time close the door. Wait just a couple of seconds and then let her out. Always use a treat and lots of praise and petting.

The rest is easy. Just keep gradually increasing the amount of time your kitty is in her carrier and don't forget the praise and treats. She'll associate the carrier with really great things and you should have no cat carrier problems.

Q: *I'd like to take my cat, Precious, with me on short car trips. So far, she howls nonstop the whole time she's in the car. How do I get her used to riding in the car?*

A: It's not unusual for cats to dislike riding in a car. Cats don't take to changes well, and most cats only get put in the car when they're going to the veterinarian. So, right away, they associate car rides with going to the vet's office and being probed and poked. I wouldn't want to get in the car either!

What you need to do is gradually accustom Precious to riding in the car and associate it with a good thing, like play or food. Always use a cat carrier when transporting Precious. I can't emphasize enough, the importance of that. Cats loose in a car can cause accidents by jumping on you while you're driving or becoming tangled under your feet or in the pedals. Cats can dart quickly out of doors or get scared and jump from your arms. Once loose, they may become frightened and dart into traffic or hide and become lost in a strange area.

Once you have gotten Precious comfortable with her carrier, start "car training" her. Start by carrying Precious, in her carrier, out to the car and then sit in the car with her, with the doors closed, for two to three minutes. While you're there, talk to her in a happy (*not reassuring*) voice and feed her little tasty treats through the grill door of her carrier. (A reassuring tone of voice reinforces her feeling that she is right to be afraid.) Then, take her back inside. That's it for the first session.

Next time, do the same, but start the car engine. Continue to talk to Precious in a relaxed, happy manner and feed her a tasty little treat about once a minute for three to five minutes. Then turn off the car and take her back inside. Give her another treat and some petting. For the next session, start the car and back it out of the driveway and then pull it back into the garage. Reward her with a food treat, then take her inside. Continue to talk to her in a happy, relaxed voice, without using a reassuring tone.

Next time, drive around the block. The time after that, drive around two blocks. Just keep gradually increasing the distance. Reward Precious with a food treat and some petting every time you come back home. She will be gradually getting used to the motion and noise of the car and will be looking forward to the petting and food treat from you.

It takes some time and effort to car train a cat this way. However, the sessions are short and cats trained this way learn to travel quietly and happily in their carriers.

Q: We've gotten our six-year-old cat where he likes to travel with us. However, he won't urinate while we're on the road. If we stay somewhere for more than about twelve hours he will go. Is that OK?

A: It is not what I would like him to do, but it's not going to hurt him occasionally to hold it until he is calm enough about the traveling to "go." Cats won't just go up to the closest tree or light post and lift a leg. They are very fastidious about their eating and elimination habits. A cat that is traveling will probably want his litter box that smells familiar to him. So . . . convenient or not, you need to take it, or one very similar to it, with some of his smell in it, along for the trip.

Many cats, even with a full bladder, won't use their litter box when you stop at the roadside rest stop. They will wait until they are in a quiet, stable environment before they feel like they can eliminate and cover it up—which is what they are used to.

The only cats this is a problem for are those with a history of feline urological syndrome. These cats should not be holding a full bladder because of their predisposition to bladder infections. This could cause a flare-up of the problem.

Q: Would you recommend tranquilizing our cat for a plane trip of about three hours?

A: I would answer based on how the cat has done in the past while traveling or while in the carrier. I personally prefer not to tranquilize if possible. Tranquilized cats must deal with the stress of travel and the stress of being drugged. I would rather you spend some time getting the cat used to traveling in her carrier and used to different sights and noises while in the carrier. If she seems to stay calm in her carrier around strange sights and sounds, there is probably no need to tranquilize her. However, if she appears stressed, or meows constantly, then Valium or Acepromazine would help ease her anxiety.

If you decide to tranquilize her, give the pill about thirty minutes before you head to the airport. This way you can be sure she is not going to have any abnormal reaction to the medication and that it is has taken effect before you board.

Q: *We are moving this summer and we will be driving for two days with our two cats in the car. What should we do to make it easier on them?*

A: Good question! You'll want to be well prepared for this trip to make it as pleasant as possible for you and the kitties.

Start well ahead of time accustoming your cats to their carriers and to riding in the car. Take your time and do it gradually. If your cats are not used to wearing collars or harnesses, start to get them used to a harness now. A harness adds another degree of safety when traveling with a cat.

Many cats don't actually throw up like dogs do, but they often drool excessively, and changes in food and water can cause diarrhea, so it's a good idea to take some paper towels and carpet cleaner in case you need to clean up. I recommend Nature's Miracle, which you can find in almost any pet store. It removes the stains and odors and can be used without diluting or mixing.

Please, make it an absolute rule to keep a harness on the cats and snap their leashes on or make sure they are closed securely in their carriers before you ever open a car door. Imagine how horrible it would be if one dashed out of the car and was lost in some totally strange location halfway between here and there. Make sure both kitties have identification tags securely attached to their collars with your name and phone numbers for your destination. (If you don't know that yet, put the name and phone number of a friend or relative. Don't forget to tell them that you've done that.) Bring along extra I.D. tags, leashes and harnesses in case of emergency.

Pack plenty of their regular food. Don't rely on buying food on the road. You may not be able to find your usual brand and the stress of changing food can add to the stress of the trip. You could end up needing *a lot* of paper towels. If you're feeding canned food, don't forget a can opener.

Pack food and water dishes, and bring along a jug of water from home. A good idea is to freeze some ice in an old, plastic butter tub with a lid on it. This allows the cat to lick and get some water, but not drink too much. On shorter trips it's also less messy. If your cats are ones that will eliminate on the har-

ness at a roadside rest, don't forget to bring along some bag-
gies so you can pick up after them. Pack their litter box and
bring along some extra litter. Don't forget a litter scoop.

Bring along a couple of catnip toys to put in their carriers
with them. Remember to pack any medications you may currently be using and bring a copy of their rabies vaccination
certificate. You may not need it, but I have seen some state
check points that ask to see current vaccination records.

Do not leave your cats in the car while you go inside a
restaurant to eat. Even on very mild days, the temperature in
a parked car can reach dangerous levels quickly due to solar
heating. (Short-faced breeds of cats such as Persians are especially vulnerable to heatstroke.) In the winter, a parked car can
quickly become very cold inside as well.

Have a good trip!

Q: *My cat is very used to riding in the car with me. She just sits on
my lap most of the time. Since she's so good in the car, do you
think she really needs a travel kennel?*

A: A travel kennel is the safest way for your cat to travel. Most cats
are not as relaxed in the car as your cat obviously is and a
travel kennel helps them stay calm and feel secure in their own
little compartment.

To answer your question, YES. I would strongly suggest a
travel kennel, even for a cat like yours, because it is safer for
her and for you. A cat loose in a car can cause an accident by
getting underfoot and interfering with the pedals, putting her
head or legs through the steering wheel and interfering with
your ability to turn quickly, or by jumping suddenly up on your
shoulder so she can see better.

Your kitty will be much safer in a kennel. In the event of an
accident, a loose cat becomes a furry flying missile and can be
badly injured, even in a minor car crash. If a door were to
come open or a window break out during an accident, she
could escape and become lost or loose in traffic. In case fire or
ambulance personnel had to retrieve your cat from an accident scene, a kennel makes the job quicker and safer.

Even if you never have an accident, a cat can slip quickly
out a door when you get out. A cat held in your arms walking

from car to building can become frightened and escape your grasp. Imagine how awful it would be for your cat to be loose in some strange neighborhood or in traffic.

For her safety, get her a carrier and use it anytime you transport her, even for short trips.

Q: *What type of travel kennel do you suggest for cats?*

A: Cats tend to feel more secure and relaxed in a more enclosed kennel while traveling, so I'd recommend the plastic type with the metal grill door.

If you think there is ever a possibility that you will want your cat to travel with you by plane, then buy the type of carrier that will fit under the airplane seat in front of you. That way your cat can travel in the cabin with you and you won't have to buy another carrier. If you don't consider flying with your cat very likely, then you may want a carrier with a little more room. Any carrier you buy should have enough room for your cat to stand up and turn around without much difficulty. Just remember that too large a carrier will allow your cat to be thrown about more in an accident.

Wire kennels are heavier than plastic, which is a downside for traveling. Although curious kitties can see everything going on when they are in a wire kennel, I find most cats don't seem to feel as secure with that much openness. They also provide no protection from the sun beating down on them through car windows, although you can cover wire kennels with a large towel.

There are soft-sided bags made for transporting cats, which are made to be carried like a shoulder bag. I don't really like these for traveling because the soft sides just kind of collapse around the cat when you set the bag down. They don't provide any protection from flying objects in the car in case of an accident. I'd also stay away from cardboard carriers, they aren't as sturdy and cats can easily chew through them.

Whatever type of kennel you get, be sure to secure the kennel with seat belts or straps to eliminate movement.

Q: *I've heard so many horror stories about pets traveling on the airlines. Is it safe?*

A: Air travel for pets is certainly safer now than it was many years ago. There is now a federal law that makes airlines responsible for the health and safety of their animal passengers. All pets must be shipped in travel kennels which meet federal regulatory standards, and a veterinary health certificate is required before any pet is accepted for a flight.

Delta Airlines was nice enough to let me spend an afternoon with them to see their pet handling process. According to their training standards, pets, in their travel kennels, are hand carried to and from the planes. They are never put on conveyor belts or baggage carousels. The pets are placed by hand in a pressurized, temperature controlled compartment, and the kennels are secured to prevent movement during turbulence. (By the way, there is no such thing as an unpressurized compartment in today's modern jets. All compartments are pressurized due to structural concerns.) The pets are checked to be sure there is adequate ventilation between kennels and that two adjacent animals aren't going to growl and snarl at each other during the trip.

Pets are not to be left out in the hot sun or cold wind. They are to be hand carried to safe places until either loading or delivery to the owner is accomplished. All airlines must follow regulations about care of the animals during layovers and must take special precautions if the weather is bad or face fines.

Even with most of the major carriers trying to better train their employees who handle animals, accidents do happen. Most pet deaths result from suffocation or heatstroke. Animals have escaped from their kennels and have been lost or killed in traffic. Pets have been sent to the wrong location and have been left out in the heat or cold.

As a cat owner, you have an advantage over owners of all but the smallest dogs in that you may be able to take your cat in the cabin with you in a special carrier designed to fit under the seat in front of you. This is certainly the safest way to go, your kitty never leaves your control. If you plan on traveling this way, make arrangements early. Most airlines limit the number of pets in a cabin to one or two. Some airlines do not allow pets to travel in the cabin at all.

If your cat must travel by air in the baggage compartment, use these safety tips to minimize the risk:

- Book a direct flight to minimize the chance of your cat ending up in the wrong location. If you must switch planes, allow plenty of time for your cat to switch planes as well.
- Book an early morning or late evening flight to avoid extreme heat. In very cold winter conditions, book a midday flight.
- Stay with your cat as long as you can before they load her. It wouldn't hurt to tip the baggage handler well.
- Freeze water in a margarine dish and attach it to the inside of the carrier so your kitty will have access to some water. By freezing the water, it won't slosh during loading, but will begin to melt by the time your cat needs it. Line the carrier with an absorbent material such as old towels or disposable diapers. This will allow spilled water or urine to be soaked up and your kitty will stay drier and more comfortable.
- For trips longer than twelve hours, attach a Baggie containing dry food to the top of the kennel with feeding instructions for airline baggage handlers.
- Put your name and phone number both on the outside of the kennel and on the inside, in case the outside tag gets torn off.
- Don't attach any tag by string or cord. It could fall into the kennel and your cat could get tangled in it and strangle. For the same reason, don't attach a leash to the kennel.

Q· *We're going to take a family vacation and we want to include the whole family—that includes our cat, Tiger. Will hotels accept cats more readily than dogs?*

A: Many hotels accept both dogs and cats. If your cat is a good traveler, she should be a nice addition to your vacation, as long as you prepare well. Because cats don't bark and disturb neighbors, many hotel managers probably don't know a cat is visiting with them.

It's a good idea to plan out where you'll stay each night well in advance and make sure each place will allow your cat to stay in the room with you. If you must leave her in the room alone for any reason, be sure to put her in her carrier and leave the thermostat set at a comfortable setting. Hang out the Do Not Disturb sign to prevent housekeeping from coming in while you are gone. This will prevent your cat from making an accidental escape. Never leave your cat tied by her leash. She could easily become entangled and strangle herself.

Not all hotels and motels allow pets. To make your planning easier, The Annenberg Communications Institute publishes a hotel and motel directory called *Pets R Permitted*. This book lists over three thousand hotels and motels that allow pets to stay with their owners, over one thousand American Boarding Kennel Association (ABKA) approved kennels for day kenneling along the way or for extended kennel stays, theme parks that accommodate pets, special veterinarian and pet-sitter location service information and travel safety and etiquette rules. (For information call (310) 217-0511.)

Q: *I'll be going overseas for four months and would like to take my cat with me. I know nothing about making these kind of arrangements. Can you help me?*

A: Traveling with your pet to a different country requires a great deal of preparation and homework. What is required will vary dramatically from country to country. You will be required to have a veterinary health certificate and a rabies vaccination certificate. The health certificate will need to be an official international health certificate and may need to be stamped and approved by the official state veterinarian. Some countries require their own special certificate and it may need to be stamped by the foreign consulate from that country. So, you'll need to check ahead with the foreign consulate for each country you wish to enter to see what will be required.

Be aware that there are some countries that require long periods of quarantine for any animal brought in. Even Hawaii, although part of the United States, requires a four-month quarantine! This is because Hawaii is rabies free and extreme steps are taken to prevent the disease from being introduced. England is one such country with strict and long quarantine restrictions.

The cost of the transport varies greatly depending on your

destination, but can be quite expensive. Your cat will be under a tremendous amount of stress on an overseas flight in a baggage compartment and will be required to spend a great deal of time in a small kennel. You should consider if the stress to your kitty and the expense incurred is worth having your furry friend with you on your trip. Remember, he may not be allowed in some hotels.

You may find that it is impossible or just not practical to take him with you overseas. If you are determined though, the services of a professional pet transportation expert can make things much simpler. They will know, or can find out, the restrictions in the countries you will be visiting and will make arrangements for your pet's transport. You can find one by looking in the phone book in most large cities.

Q: *My husband and I will be going on vacation for three weeks. I'm very concerned about my cats. I've never kenneled them before. Is it safe to kennel at cat? How can I tell if a kennel is a good one?*
A: These are good questions. It's always hard to leave pets in the care of strangers. I know it is for me. If you've decided that kenneling is your best option, then plan way ahead and visit several kennels to find the best. It's always a good idea to ask other cat-loving friends if they have used any kennels and how their experience was.

Personally visit each kennel you are considering. Visit unannounced and be sure to see where the cats are kept. Some facilities may say they can't show you anything past the reception room due to insurance restrictions. Don't put your cats in any kennel that won't show you the entire facility.

The kennel area should be clean and fairly odor free. You'll want a kennel that will feed your kitties their usual brand of food, even if you must supply their food. They should ask you how often your cat is usually fed.

Make sure the cages are large enough for the cat to stretch out and be comfortable without sleeping in his litter box.

The kennel area should be temperature controlled at all times and the cat kennel area should be separate from the area where the dogs are kenneled.

Make sure the kennel area looks secure in the event of an escaped cat. If a cat were to escape from its cage (which happens), it shouldn't then be able to easily escape from the facility. Double doors and a high perimeter fence are safety factors.

The kennel should have you fill out a questionnaire with the location and phone number where you will be as well as that of a friend or family member. They should note your cat's regular veterinarian and her phone number. They should require proof of vaccinations. This is important. Remember, if they don't require proof from you, then they don't require it from anybody else either.

I like kennels that allow you to bring an object from home with your smell on it to put in kitty's cage with her, such as an old T-shirt. (Don't wash it first.) I also like to bring a couple of favorite toys for kitty.

Visit a number of facilities well in advance. By comparison, you'll be able to decide the best choice. Make reservations early. It's a good idea to have a friend stop by and check on your cats while you're gone.

Q: *Our family will be taking a camping trip this summer. We usually take our dog with us and we were wondering about taking our cat. She is used to a harness and leash and we were thinking she could be tethered just like our dog. What do you think?*

A: I understand your not wanting to leave your cat behind, but I can think of a lot of inherent dangers for her on a camping trip.

First of all, you never want to tether a cat unsupervised for *any* length of time. Many cats have choked after getting tangled in tie-out lines. It can happen very quickly. Tethered cats are also unable to escape from attacking dogs or other animals.

If she should get loose, she may become frightened and take off. In the great outdoors, you may never find her and she is ill equipped to survive without you.

For her safety, and your peace of mind, I'd suggest you do this trip without her.

CHAPTER 3

Humane Societies, Abused Cats and Strays

A wonderful example of humanitarianism and teaching children proper values is seen in this story relayed to me on my show by a fourth-grade teacher:

"Dr. Jim, I have to tell you about an experience I had along with my fourth-grade class. Coming into school one day, a child in my class came across a very sick, very neglected cat. Against my better judgment he brought it into class and we had a long discussion about what to do. We decided to get Mr. Friday back on his feet as a class project. I got the principal's permission and I agreed to foster the little guy in my home.

Well, to make a long story short, the kids worked to raise money for veterinary bills, food, medications and supplies. The children made toys for him and showed such love and compassion toward this little kitten. Mr. Friday pulled even rival children together in their quest to get him well and adoptable. We even made the morning news.

Mr. Friday did get back on his feet, and my class has learned lessons about responsibility, team work, compassion and love. Mr. Friday was the best teacher I've ever seen. He was adopted into a very nice family, and we hope they will bring him by every now and then so the children can keep up with their pal."

Cats offer so much love and companionship. It's terribly sad to realize how many cats have no caring and responsible home to share this love with. As many as twelve million cats a year end up in animal shelters. Only about 17% of these cats will eventually be adopted, mostly kittens. Adoption rates for adult cats are very low. Unadopted cats must be euthanized to make room for new stray and homeless cats. Added to these statistics are staggering numbers of feral (wild stray) cats that live and die tragic lives on the streets without ever making it to a humane society or shelter.

The single biggest culprit in this tragic problem of pet over-population is the irresponsible pet owner who will not spay or neuter his cat. Two uncontrolled breeding cats are capable of producing as many as 80,399,780 kittens in just ten years!

Abandoned cats are another alarming problem. Some people mistakenly think that cats are able to fend for themselves, and they abandon their pets once the novelty of kittenhood wears off. Homeless cats live tragic and short lives on the street, being prime targets for starvation, disease and death from cars, dogs and other predators. Homeless cats are especially susceptible to abuse from cruel people and are sometimes trapped and sold to research facilities.

While humane societies do their best to care for homeless pets, they are typically overcrowded, understaffed and woefully under-financed for the numbers of animals that come through their doors. Over 80% of all cats that end up in shelters and humane societies will eventually be euthanized.

There are simply not enough homes for all these cats.

Q: *I would like to do something to help the cat overpopulation problem. What can one person do?*

A: There are ways to help. The most important is to *spay* or *neuter* your pets. Try to encourage your friends and acquaintances to do the same. In addition to this there are ways that individuals can make a difference. If you're looking for a new pet, consider saving a life. Adopt a cat or kitten from a shelter or humane society. Rescue a homeless, abused or neglected cat, or adopt an older cat. These kitties that have had a rough start often seem to realize and appreciate how lucky they are. My experience has been that they make some of the most wonderful pets.

Q: *There is a stray cat living in a vacant lot near where I work. I would like to help her but I can't get close to her. I've thought about trapping her. What do you think?*

A: Before you try to catch this cat, you need to decide what you're going to do with her once you have caught her. If you are not able to keep her yourself, you'll need to try to find her a home. If she is an abandoned or lost pet, you may be able to get her to come to you with some time and persistence. If she is feral (wild) it may be difficult to tame her unless she is a young kitten, under about twelve weeks old.

You could call your local animal control to trap her, but feral cats are not usually considered real adoptable and chances are she will end up being euthanized. A humane society or a no-kill shelter in your area will be able to offer you advice in trapping her and can probably loan you a humane trap.

Make sure that she is not a nursing mother before you trap her. If you trap a nursing female and leave her kittens behind, they will certainly die without her care. Look for indications of nursing, such as protruding nipples and full milk sacs.

Don't try to pick her up with your bare hands. She could bite or scratch out of fear. Wear long sleeves and pants and use thick gloves when capturing her.

Q: *My friend and I have been trying to catch a wild cat that is living under the building where we work. What advice can you give us for after we catch her?*

A: Once you catch her, take her to your veterinarian right away. She will need to be tested for infectious diseases, vaccinated and spayed. Be sure not to introduce her to any cats you already own until she has been given a clean bill of health. If you explain that you are rescuing this kitty off the street, some veterinarians will give you some discount on vaccinating and spaying her.

Be prepared for this kitty to take some time to become comfortable with you and your home. She may have had little contact with humans, or worse yet, may have been abused. It can take weeks, months or longer for feral cats to learn to trust and accept handling from humans. If you don't have the personality or patience for this type of rehabilitation, try to find a loving home for her or try to place her in a no-kill shelter that will work to rehabilitate her. Very busy households with young children and lots of other pets may not be suitable. If you choose to keep her yourself, you'll no doubt find a lot of satisfaction in watching her come out of her shell and learn to trust you.

Q: *I currently have five wonderful house cats and cannot possibly adopt any more. However, there are three stray cats that hang around my neighborhood and the woods behind it. I put food out for them on a regular basis, but I want to do something to help them. They keep having litters of kittens, which never seem to live long. Do you have any suggestions?*

A: The first thing I'd suggest is talking to your veterinarian and seeing if he would give you a discount on spaying and neutering all three. They should be also be vaccinated and checked for infectious diseases. If you talk to him ahead of time and explain the situation, he may give you a break on his fees. Your veterinarian or local humane society may then be able to help you find homes for the cats. You can also try finding homes for them yourself, but be careful not to give away a rescued cat for free to someone you don't know. There are people who sell these cats to research laboratories.

If you can't find homes for the cats, then have them spayed or neutered, vaccinated and checked for infectious diseases then turn them loose in their territory again. If you plan to release them again, tell your veterinarian. He will want to use dissolving sutures and will probably give each cat a long-acting antibiotic shot. Continue to feed the cats on a regular basis and you'll have at least prevented any further litters and given them a healthy chance.

Q: *I volunteer at a no-kill shelter. I have fallen in love with a sweet, yellow tabby male who was abused by his former owner. He is very loving, but scares very easily. He is especially afraid of men. Do you think he would make a good pet?*

A: It takes patience and understanding to help an abused cat learn to trust people again and become a loving pet. You need to understand this going into it. How much emotional damage the cat has suffered depends on the type and degree of abuse he was exposed to. Since you can get him to come to you in the shelter, then you should eventually be able to get him to trust you to handle him at home.

Cats that are merely timid and afraid are usually able to learn to trust again. Cats that are extremely aggressive toward humans are very difficult to rehabilitate and are not good candidates for pets.

Before you adopt him, ask yourself some questions. Do you have the patience and the personality to provide the care needed to help him overcome his fear? Is your home environment suitable? A noisy house with lots of visitors, many pets or small children would be very difficult for a traumatized cat. Will everyone in the household want this cat and be willing to help it? He certainly doesn't need any further negative experiences with humans. Will he be able to be an indoor-only cat?

If you decide to adopt him, you need to make a commitment to stick it out. It can take time to help an abused cat recover, but it is well worth the effort.

Q: *I have decided to adopt a young adult cat that was abandoned by his previous owners. He may have been abused; he is very timid of strangers. What can I do to help him adjust?*

A: When you bring the cat home, let him stay in a quiet room by himself with his food, water, litter box and some toys. Don't worry if he spends most of his time hiding. Being in a new environment is scary for most cats, but especially for an abandoned or abused cat. You can go in to visit him often, but don't force your attention on him. Just sit quietly and talk to him. It will probably take him several days or weeks to become accustomed to his room and your voice and smell.

Definitely keep other pets and small children away from him until he is comfortable with his room and with you. Once he seems comfortable in his room, you can let him out to take short explorations of the house. Be sure to leave his door open so he can rush back to his room if he feels the need. Patience, patience, patience is the key. Don't rush him into anything.

As he becomes comfortable leaving his room and exploring the house, you can move his food and water bowl and litter box just a few steps at a time toward their permanent location. That way he can find them easily.

Introduce him gradually to new things and to other pets. Try to be sensitive to things he is especially fearful of. For instance, if he panics and runs every time he sees a broom, put him in his room before you sweep the kitchen.

A friendly, well-adjusted companion cat is often very helpful in helping an abused cat adjust. The companionship of another cat is reassuring to many abused cats and observing the other cat's interactions with you may help your new cat learn to trust you. Some cats prefer to be loners, however, and another cat in the house may increase the stress.

Most of all, just give him time, kindness and patience. Once they learn to trust you, cats who have had a rough start in life seem to be especially appreciative of their new homes.

Q: *We wanted to adopt a kitten from the local humane society, but they began asking so many questions, it offended us. Many of the questions were personal. They refused to let us adopt a kitten because we wanted it to be an outdoor cat. Is this normal procedure?*

A: Don't be offended. Everything you just told me indicates that this is a highly responsible humane society with excellent rules for adoption. Good humane societies realize that the chances for a successful adoption are directly related to a successful match between adopted cat and responsible new owner.

These humane societies typically have a long questionnaire to fill out, including questions about the age and number of family members, other pets in the home and size of house. They also ask about your previous experience with pets, what type of pets you have had and what has happened to them if they are not still with you. You may think these extreme measures, but they're really not. Cats and kittens that end up in humane societies have already been through a rough time. Although their basic needs are met while there, they don't have the security and comfort of a "home." They are deprived of the special attention that comes with being someone's special pet. There's a very good chance that kittens will recover quickly from their deprived beginnings if they get adopted to a good home, where they will fit well into the family life style.

The last thing these kittens need is to be adopted to a home, then returned to the shelter once the cuteness of kittenhood has worn off. Once a cat is past kittenhood, it's chance of being adopted is very slim.

The humane society staffers will know that outdoor cats typically live very short lives due to exposure to disease and all the dangers that befall a cat outdoors. By questioning you, they are attempting to assure that any cat you adopt will have the best chance for a happy and healthy life. They are also able to eliminate people who would be unable to properly care for a cat, either because they lack the proper facilities or don't have the financial resources to assure proper food, shelter and veterinary care.

Q: *We went into a humane society the other day looking for a kitten. The smell almost knocked us over and the people there acted as if we were bothering them. We left not wanting to adopt a kitten from them, but knowing there were many homeless cats in bad conditions there. Should they be reported?*

A: Yes. While most humane societies are well run and staffed by caring, knowledgeable people, there are certainly some with problems.

Most humane societies, even well run ones, are trying to care for more animals than their facilities can comfortably handle. This is because the pet overpopulation problem is so overwhelming. Most humane societies are also chronically short of funds because a good portion of their operating expenses must come from donations. Volunteers usually make up a part of the staff at any humane society and this can result in unpredictable reception and responses to questions. For these reasons, I like to give each of these humane societies the benefit of the doubt. There are, however, some which are just poorly run and clearly not doing a good job of caring for and adopting out pets.

I do think you should report what your experience was on your visit. You may need to do a little investigating in order to find the best authority to report to. First, try to contact the chairman of the humane society's board of directors. If the humane society is city-owned, you can report them to the mayor's office or the city council.

Q: *A friend of mine is a member of a large national animal rights group. She is trying to get me to join her at some of the group's protests. I believe in humane treatment of animals, but these people are frankly a little far out in left field. What do you think?*

A: Most animal rights groups started out with the best intentions. However, with the tightening of the economy, contributions to all types of charities are down nationwide. As these groups compete for shrinking donations, many of them have resorted to sensationalistic, headline-grabbing tactics.

If you don't agree with all the stands taken by your friend's group, by all means don't support them, either by your presence or your donations. Only by supporting groups that represent your beliefs will animal humane groups get back on track.

If you'd like to do something to help animals, I strongly suggest volunteering and donating money at your community level. The pet overpopulation problem accounts for the needless destruction of over fifteen and a half million dogs and cats every year. Local humane societies tend to focus on this important problem. They work tirelessly educating the public to spay and neuter, and adopting homeless pets. A good number of the national groups ignore this problem altogether, focusing instead on sensationalism that will attract media attention. If you are not comfortable with your friend's organization, you may want to keep your donations of time and money closer to home.

CHAPTER 4

Declawing

"Agnes was over the other day playing with our big tom cat, Charles. She was talking to me and had touched me on the arm about the time she touched Charles on a sore spot. He clawed her pretty good and she did me, too. After the excitement, Agnes had a couple of deep scratches the shape of Charles' paw, and I had a couple in the shape of Agnes' hand. I wonder if we can get Charles declawed?"

There is no absolute answer to whether declawing should be done or not. Some cats need it, most don't. No one can deny the fact that if allowed to do as they will with their claws, cats can scratch people and destroy furniture with those very sharp appendages.

My major objection to declawing is that it is done too often, and too quickly, without ever trying to teach the cat to use its claws appropriately. Owners begin to see this rather drastic surgery as routine, something normally done. "We've brought Fluffy in for her shots, deworming and, oh yeah, declaw her while she's here."

The problem with declawing cats is that it is unnatural. The surgery is severe, fraught with complications and is often performed improperly even by otherwise very good veterinarians. Deprived of their natural means of defense, many declawed cats become biters.

Although there are cases where a cat needs to be declawed, most cats, when given the chance, will learn to use their claws when it is appropriate, and keep them safely tucked away when it is not appropriate. Not every cat should be a candidate for this severe surgery.

Q: *We adopted a cat that had all four paws declawed. We notice she has a tendency to bite a lot more than usual. Could this have anything to do with being declawed?*

A: Declawed cats have a greater tendency to bite than cats with their natural claws. Because their major tool for protection and grasping has been taken away, these cats feel somewhat insecure. Since biting is their only remaining defense, these cats often learn to give a warning bite to let everyone know they still have their teeth.

The problem is that they get scolded for this, many times harshly, which only accelerates the aggression. The cat feels even more in need of defending itself by biting.

Your cat can be trained out of this. It will take some time and patience and everyone in your home must cooperate with the training. Chapter 13, Behavior Problems and Aggression, addresses how to teach a cat not to bite.

Q: *We had our cat declawed last week and she has been picking at her feet ever since. Now she has one paw bleeding and we think we can see bone sticking out. What do we do?*

A: Get her to your veterinarian right away. You may very well see bone sticking out. When a cat is declawed, if the procedure is done properly, the most distant finger bone (distal phalanx) is actually separated from the middle finger bone. If the end or middle bone is cut instead of separated because the doctor used dog's nail trimmers for the surgery (a practice frowned upon by most surgeons), then a piece of bone can stick out through the skin. The skin is not healing as it should because this rough piece of bone irritates the surgical opening. This is an invitation to bone infection and permanent problems with the cat's foot.

The doctor will need to carefully examine, perhaps X-ray, the foot to see what exactly is going on. Correction will be based on the findings. It may simply need resuturing if the cat has just licked the surgical wound open. It could also be a major problem. Don't waste time, get her in.

Q: *Our cat was declawed last year, yet today we noticed a claw growing out of her front left paw. It is coming out crooked and looks bad. Why is that?*

A: To properly declaw a cat, the distal digit must be entirely separated from the rest of the foot. This removes the entire bone and all the germinal tissue with it. This germinal tissue is the part of the bone responsible for growing claw.

When doctors use a dog's nail trimmer for the surgical procedure, instead of a scalpel blade, many times that piece of germinal tissue is left behind only to grow into an aberrant claw later in life. This little bit of bone is also responsible for pain, bone infections and other problems after the operation. Some doctors have perfected a technique for using the nail trimmers and do so properly. However, many have not and get away with a barbaric attempt at surgery using the device. The American Animal Hospital Association has published and approved the scalpel method for declawing. They discourage the use of such trimmers, and so do I.

Q: *Our cat is walking very tenderly on her front paws. We had her declawed two weeks ago. Shouldn't she be healed by now?*

A: Yes. If she is limping due to pain, then the surgery was either poorly done, has become infected or there is some other complication from the surgery. Some cats limp initially because of the pain after surgery and simply learn to walk like that to get attention. However, this is very un-catlike and very rare in my experience. Most of the time, limping two weeks or more after a declaw surgery is due to a problem. Take her in to the doctor again and investigate the source of the complication.

Q: *My husband just bought some new leather furniture and is now insisting I declaw my two cats. They are five and nine and have never caused a problem before. What do I do?*

A: I would not declaw them. If there were a history of destroying furniture, I could see where he would have a concern. However, because they are so good, why run the risk of surgical complications, anesthetic risks and compensatory behavior problems with declawing mature, well-behaved cats?

In order to keep the peace at your house, I would make sure the cats don't decide to mark the lovely new furniture that has suddenly appeared in your home by reinforcing the use of a scratching post for a few days. Play with them at the post, rub some fresh catnip on the post or hang a new catnip toy from the post. Most importantly, praise the cats for scratching on the post. You might also head to the pet store and buy some pet repellent spray, such as Repel. You can spray the furniture directly, or spray a towel and lay it on the furniture. You would need to respray daily for about two weeks to establish a habit of the cats staying away from your husband's prized new furniture.

Q: *My elderly mother and my two-year-old daughter have both been scratched by our cat. Nicki is not being mean, she's just very playful. What do you think about declawing Nicki? I'd like my daughter and mother to be able to play with her without being injured.*

A: If ever there was a perfect case for declawing, you're it. Although I am generally against declawing cats, you may have good reasons for the surgery. Your daughter is too young to be taught to always handle the cat just right. Therefore, she is clearly susceptible to being scratched either while playing with the cat or because she mishandles the cat.

Since elderly people often have more fragile skin which tears easily and heals with more difficulty, you certainly don't want your mother to be scratched.

If your cat is still a kitten, she may just not have learned yet to keep her claws in while playing with people. If you keep her claws well trimmed and supervise interactions between her and your daughter, that may solve the problem.

If you decide to have her declawed, she will need to be an indoor-only cat. A cat's front claws are its main defense as well as its tools for climbing and escaping danger. You should also be aware that declawed cats have a greater tendency to bite, since their primary means of defending themselves has been taken away. So, it will still be necessary to supervise interactions between your cat and your daughter.

A declaw procedure, done properly by an up-to-date, competent surgeon, has few complications, and recovery is within a few days. Check with your veterinarian and make sure he uses the scalpel procedure to declaw.

Q: *I have really tried to teach my cat to use a scratching post, but she still scratches my furniture. I love my kitty but I can't have her destroying my house. What can I do?*

A: If you have truly tried to teach your cat to use a scratching post and have done all you can to make the furniture unappealing to her, then you may have one of those rare cats that simply won't listen to reason. In this case, declawing may be your only recourse.

Although declawing will stop the furniture destruction, there are some factors you will need to consider. Your cat will need to stay inside at all times as she will have no real way to defend herself from danger. Without claws, she will also be hampered in climbing and escaping danger.

Seek out the best veterinarian you can find to do the surgery. I emphasize this because I have seen so many botched jobs of declawing cats. I guess this surgery is seen as menial by some doctors and they simply don't spend the time necessary to do the job right.

I don't see a problem with asking over the phone if a doctor uses the scalpel method or the nail trimmer method. I would definitely go with the doctor who has taken the time to learn the more sophisticated procedure using a scalpel blade. Some doctors can properly declaw a cat with dog's nail trimmers, but the margin for error is narrow and complications are more common with this method.

If you have friends who have had cats successfully declawed with no complications, get a referral. Let the doctor know ahead of time that you are concerned about postsurgical complications and ask him to explain everything he does to minimize problems.

Do good postsurgical after care at home and be sure the veterinarian sees your cat a week after surgery to check for complications.

CHAPTER 5

Senior Cats

"Our family cat is nineteen years old. She'll be twenty in two months. We've listened to your radio show for the past six years, and we think your advice is great. We're thinking of having a birthday party for her and we want you to be the guest of honor!"

As veterinary medicine advances, just as with human medicine, more pet cats are living longer. This is especially true for cats who are kept indoors. While the majority of outdoor cats live less than three years, well-cared-for indoor cats can easily live into their middle teens or even twenties. There are many documented cases of cats living well into their upper twenties and even into their thirties, although this is certainly not the norm.

Just as with humans, advancing age brings changes to a cat's biological systems. As owners of older cats, we need to make some adjustments to their care in order to ensure they remain healthy and happy in their senior years. Older cats need some special attention and care that requires a degree of devotion on your part. However, it is a small price to pay for the companionship and love your pet gives you.

Q: *Our fourteen-year-old cat, Zach, hissed and scratched our eight-year-old granddaughter the other day when the child picked him up while he was sleeping. What do you think caused that?*

A: Just as with many people, a lot of cats become a bit grouchy as they get older. It is not at all unusual for senior cats to become less tolerant of being handled by strangers, and especially children, who tend to be rougher and louder than adults. This is very understandable when you think about it. Older cats sleep more soundly than they did when they were young. They're less aware of what's going on around them and are, therefore, easy to startle if awakened suddenly.

Senior cats tend to stay very loving and affectionate to their families. They just become less tolerant of any rough handling, strangers, noise or commotion. That makes sense. Elderly humans don't care much for any of that either.

It would be a very good idea to call a family meeting and let everyone, especially any children, know that Zach is a senior citizen and deserves a certain amount of respect and special care. Lay the law down that he is to be handled gently and not bothered while he is sleeping, eating or in his litter box. That should prevent further problems.

Q: *Our veterinarian says our sixteen-year-old Persian is overweight. She weighs the same now as she did when she was young, and he didn't think she was overweight then. What do you think?*

A: If your cat weighs as much now as she did in her prime, she may be overweight. Many healthy older cats weigh somewhat less as they age, although they shouldn't exhibit a sudden weight loss unless they're put on a diet.

Obesity is the most common nutritional disease in dogs and cats. Both dogs and cats that are obese run a much higher risk of diabetes, cardiac problems and risks associated with anesthesia and surgery. Obesity drastically shortens the life of your cat.

Your veterinarian is right on target and is giving you good advice. Follow his recommendations and decrease your kitty's weight. She'll be healthier and more active, and she'll live longer!

Q: *My veterinarian says my fifteen-year-old Manx, Hemingway, is becoming a couch potato. He has put him on a reducing diet. Isn't it normal for older cats to be less active and heavier than when they were young?*

A: Yes, it's normal for a cat's activity level to slow down as he ages, but you don't want to let him get overweight. It's important for his health that he stay active and at a good weight. Besides decreasing the amount of food that Hemingway eats, you need to increase his activity level. Encourage him to play for ten to fifteen minutes every day.

You can make a wonderful cat toy using an old fishing pole with a string and a piece of cloth tied to the end. It works great at getting even older, sedentary cats up and moving. Besides helping him lose weight, daily exercise will help keep Hemingway's joints and muscles in good shape, as well as his respiratory and cardiovascular systems.

Q: *My eleven-year-old female calico has been diagnosed with mammary cancer. My veterinarian says this rarely affects cats that have been spayed. Is this true?*

A: It is true. Cats spayed before their first heat cycle are hundreds of times less likely to develop breast cancer later in life. Now that she has the disease, the doctor will likely remove the cancerous tissue and spay her as well. This decreases the likelihood that any hormones are produced which would make the problem worsen over the remainder of her lifetime.

Q: *I have a seventeen-year-old kitty. He has always kept himself immaculately groomed until the last year. Now he doesn't seem to groom much and his coat gets oily and smells bad. I hate to have to bathe him at his age. Is there any other way to get his fur clean?*

A: First, I'd like you to have your kitty checked by your veterinarian to make sure there is not a medical reason for his oily coat and odor. An oily coat is a symptom sometimes seen with hyperthyroidism, a prominent illness among older cats. If your veterinarian rules out health problems, then we can consider this an age-related grooming problem.

As cats get older, up into their late teens and early twenties, they may become less able to do a good job of grooming themselves. It is up to you to help your cat stay well groomed, both for his comfort and his health. (He'll look better as well.)

A daily brushing will keep his coat free of mats and dirt and help distribute the oils along the hair shaft. Most cats begin to really enjoy being brushed and look forward to the daily grooming.

If there is no flea problem and the coat is simply oily and not excessively dirty, you can try using a dry shampoo to clean the coat. They work well to remove dirt and leave the coat smelling fresh if you use them properly. It is important to work the powder well into the coat and then brush it out very thoroughly. Work from rear of cat forward, powdering a section and then brushing it out thoroughly before moving on to the next section. One nice benefit to dry shampoos is that you can do part of the cat at a time and can break the job up into three or four short sessions over a couple of days. You can buy dry shampoos from your pet store or make your own by mixing one part baby powder to three parts cornstarch.

If your cat has fleas, he will probably need a bath and perhaps a dip. It's okay to bathe older kitties occasionally as long as you are careful. The key in bathing all cats, but especially senior cats, is to prepare well ahead of time and have all your bathing tools ready before you start so that you can make the whole process as quick as possible. Make sure to use warm water, but don't use water as hot as you would bathe in. Cats, especially older cats, cannot tolerate water that's hot and may become overheated. Use lukewarm water. Pick a warm day or make sure the house is warm so that kitty doesn't get chilled. After kitty is toweled off, wrap him in a dry towel and hold him until he warms up. Make sure the house stays nice and warm until he is completely dry.

Q: *I've heard you talk about the importance of diet in senior cats. My Persian, Lady Di, is in good health but she's fourteen now. What would be the best diet for her?*

A: First, eliminate table scraps and human food "treats" from Lady Di's diet, no matter how much she loves them. Even small amounts of table scraps can become a significant percentage of a cat's diet. This can upset the balance of fats, proteins, carbohydrates, vitamins and minerals she needs to be healthy.

For a healthy older cat, I recommend a premium brand. You

should feed a commercial diet that meets all her nutritional
needs and a few other very important criteria:

1. The diet should be low in magnesium to help prevent the
   common urinary disease called feline urological syndrome,
   or FUS.
2. It should create an acid urine when excreted, again to prevent FUS.
3. It should be meat based, as cats are true carnivores and only
   animal-based ingredients contain enough taurine, vitamin A
   and arachidonic acid to properly supply these things to our
   domestic cats who do not kill and eat prey animals.
4. Finally it should be palatable in order to convince the cat to
   eat it.

Because her appetite is probably still really good, but she's
not as active as she used to be, she needs a food with fewer
calories but the proper balance of nutrients of the highest quality. I recommend Science Diet Feline Maintenance Light, or
Nature's Recipe Optimum Feline Diet Lite or Iams Less Active
for Cats.

If your cat does *not* have a history of FUS or other disease
and the expense of the premium brands is a problem, then the
better grocery-store brands are what I recommend.

When asked on talk radio about which grocery-store brands
I recommend for cats, I primarily recommend Alpo's cat food
because of the extensive research that went into the formula. I
have also personally seen the high level of quality control at
their plant.

Q: *It seems that since our Siamese has been getting older he doesn't
hear as well. Could he be going deaf?*
A: Your kitty could be experiencing some hearing loss as he ages.
However, hearing loss can also be caused by ear infections, wax
buildup in the ears or buildup of dirt in the ear canals. Have your
veterinarian check your cat to rule out a possible medical problem.

Keep your kitty's ears clean by moistening a cotton ball with
ear cleansing solution (available at your pet store) and gently

swabbing the part of the ear that you can easily see. Don't probe down into the ear canal. It is very easy to damage the delicate ear drum. Make a habit of checking your kitty's ears when you brush him, and clean them whenever they have any dirt buildup.

If everything checks out OK at your veterinarian's office and it does turn out to be an age-related hearing loss, remember this when you are around your cat. Cats with hearing loss adjust very well. They compensate by learning to use sight and their sense of vibration more. Just be careful when approaching your cat from behind or when he's napping. You don't want to startle him. Move slowly around him and try to catch his attention before you reach out and touch him.

Q: *What should we do about our Abyssinian's bad breath? It seems to be so much worse since he's gotten older. He's fifteen now.*

A: Have your Abyssinian checked by your veterinarian. Bad breath may be a symptom of periodontal disease, a common problem among middle-aged and older cats. Cats tend to get subgingival erosions, which mean the teeth decay just below the gumline and that may not be obvious when you look at your cat's mouth.

Periodontal disease may occur in as many as 80% of all cats over five years of age. Untreated, it can lead to infections that may damage the heart, liver and kidneys. Many cat's lives are shortened by such infections that could have been prevented had the owner had the cat checked by a veterinarian when the bad breath was first noticed.

To prevent these problems from occurring, older cats need their teeth cleaned more often to remove tartar buildup. This needs to be done by your veterinarian and usually is done under anesthesia. You don't want your older kitty to have to go under anesthesia any more than absolutely necessary, so you need to keep tartar buildup to a minimum by cleaning the teeth at home between cleanings by your veterinarian. You need to clean the teeth at least twice a week, using a special cat toothbrush and a special toothpaste designed for pets. Your veterinarian can show you how.

Q: *My wife and I have a fifteen-year-old Turkish Van. Sue has been coughing a lot and seems short of breath often. What do you think might cause this?*

A: There are a number of conditions which might cause your cat's symptoms, from allergies or asthma, to congestive heart failure. When dealing with an older cat, especially, you should call your veterinarian as soon as you notice *any* change in your cat's health. While some problems may not be serious, others could indicate serious conditions that can progress quickly if not treated. Take Sue in for a checkup right away.

Q: *My husband and I have a five-year-old Devon Rex. He is the most wonderful cat, with so much personality. We want to do everything possible to ensure he lives as long and as healthy a life as possible. I hear of cats living into their late twenties. Do these owners do anything special to keep their cats so healthy?*

A: Yes, I'm sure they do. A healthy cat in his late twenties has definitely been well cared for. I'll give you my short prescription for making your cat's life as healthy and as long as possible.

- Keep your cat indoors at all times. The great outdoors is a very dangerous place for cats. The average life span of an outdoor cat is less than three years, while the average life span of an indoor cat is thirteen years. Cats that live indoors, but are allowed to go outdoors at times, are at even greater risk, because they are less streetwise. Cats can live happy, fulfilled and long lives indoors.

- Spay or neuter your cat at six months of age, or as soon as you can if you adopt an adult cat. Spayed and neutered cats are at decreased risk of some serious health problems as compared to their intact feline friends. You can essentially eliminate your cat's chances of developing mammary cancer by spaying her before her first heat cycle.

- Be diligent about vaccinations. Veterinary medical advances have made it possible to vaccinate against many of the diseases that have killed large numbers of cats in the not too distant past. Your cat can't be protected though, if it's not vaccinated.

- Feed your cat the highest-quality food you can buy, formulated for its stage in life. I recommend one of the super-premium brands, such as Hill's Science Diet, Nature's Recipe or Iams cat food. Many of the diseases we veterinarians see in cats are caused by poor nutrition.

- Don't let your cat become overweight. Obesity causes major health problems for senior cats and can dramatically shorten a cat's life span.
- Keep your kitty active. Make it a habit to get the fishing pole toy (described previously in this chapter) or catnip mouse out and play with kitty for ten or fifteen minutes every night before you go to bed. An active kitty is a healthy kitty and is less likely to become overweight. A companion cat may help your cat stay more active.
- Develop a relationship with a good veterinarian and take kitty in for yearly checks at vaccination time. Have kitty checked more often as he gets into his teens. Many illnesses in older cats can be successfully treated if caught early.

Q: *We have a sixteen-year-old mixed-breed cat, Jasmine. Lately she seems to catch her claws in the carpet as she walks. Could she be having trouble retracting her claws?*

A: As cats get older, their claws become thicker and are more likely to become torn. This makes them easier to catch on carpet or upholstery.

Check Jasmine's claws and make sure none are torn or jagged. Keep her claws trimmed every week to ensure they don't become too long. I like to use human nail trimmers to trim cat's claws. Most cats have light-colored claws and you can easily see where the "quick" or blood vessel ends. Just trim well below the quick, taking off only the sharp point of the claw. You can also take an emery board or nail file and smooth the ends of the claws once you've trimmed them. This will keep her claws from catching.

Q: *Our Maine Coon, Max, is six years old and is starting to become noticeably less active. Do you think it would be a good idea to get him a new kitty friend?*

A: Yes, one of the best ways to keep an cat active, happy and, therefore, healthier is to get him a young cat as a companion and playmate. You'll notice a big difference in his activity level once he has adjusted to the new addition.

Use caution and common sense in adding a new cat to the family. Obviously, a cat in its twenties is a very senior citizen and will have a much decreased activity level. A cat of this age won't enjoy or tolerate a rambunctious kitten very well. At that age, he will prefer as few changes as possible and a new cat may mean more stress than anything else.

A younger to middle-aged cat, say four years to twelve years of age should be able to adjust to a new friend. It can take some time for your established cat to fully accept the newcomer, sometimes months, but once he does I think you'll see a happier, more active cat. A kitten or cat of the opposite sex is usually accepted the best by an older cat. It also helps if the cat is spayed or neutered if it is over six months old. (See Chapter 11 for tips on introducing a new pet to an established pet.)

Q: *My fourteen-year-old cat has lost a lot of weight over the last two months. She is being very active and seems to have a better appetite than usual. Do I need to worry about her weight loss?*

A: Yes, weight loss in an older cat can be a sign of serious medical problems. Her weight loss, combined with her high activity level and increased appetite may be signs of hyperthyroidism, a condition common in older cats. Have her checked by your veterinarian right away. Many medical problems in older cats are able to be treated quite successfully if caught in time.

Q: *Our old kitty, Frisky, is getting on in years. What special preventive measures should we take to keep him healthy, and how often should he see the vet?*

A: Frisky should now be checked by your veterinarian *every six months*. Due to the fact that cats age at a more rapid rate than humans, significant changes to your cat's vital systems can occur in as little as three to six months as he gets older. In addition to his veterinary checkups, here are some important points about caring for Frisky in his senior years.

• Keep Frisky's weight at a good level and encourage him to get some exercise every day. Ten to fifteen minutes of the fishing pole toy or chasing a catnip mouse on a string will help him stay active and healthy. This will keep his muscles, joints and cardiovascular systems in good shape. An active kitty is a healthier kitty.

• Frisky may need more help with his grooming as he gets older. Pay special attention to his teeth. Tooth problems are common in older cats and can cause other health problems if left untreated. Your veterinarian will need to clean his teeth more often and you will need to brush them twice a week at home.

• Check for lumps and bumps on his body when grooming. These may be tumors, which may be benign or malignant. If you find a lump on Frisky, don't wait to see what it does, take him immediately to your veterinarian.

• Remember that older cats are less tolerant of heat or cold. Keep Frisky in the house and leave the air conditioner on in very warm weather or leave a fan blowing where he can get in front of it. In the winter, keep him inside the house and make sure he has a warm kitty bed to get into.

• Give him lots of love and affection. Try to keep his routine fairly consistent. As he gets older, he will become less tolerant of change and will feel more secure with a stable routine. Let everyone in the family know they need to interact with Frisky a little differently now that he is getting older. Many senior cats don't "look their age" and children, especially, may try to play with him as if he were young.

CHAPTER 6

Euthanasia and Pet Loss

Don't be dismayed at good-byes. A farewell is necessary
before you can ever meet again. And meeting again, after
moments or lifetimes, is certain for those who are friends.
Richard Bach from *Illusions*

Because pets give us companionship, loyalty and unconditional love, they become a big part of our daily lives. It is understandable then, that it is so difficult when a cherished pet dies. Since pets can mean so much to us and we can grow to love them so much, the grief we experience after the death of a pet can seem staggering. In truth, the grief process is exactly the same as when we lose a very close human friend. The feelings of loss, emptiness and loneliness are just the same.

One of the most difficult decisions a pet owner can face is whether it is time to end a pet's suffering through humane euthanasia. As a veterinarian and talk show host, I have helped hundreds of clients and listeners face this decision. It is never easy.

Q: *I lost my Abyssinian cat, Tabatha, three weeks ago. I'm having a*
real hard time getting over this. The hardest part is that none of
my friends seem to understand why I'm still so upset over losing
a pet.

A: I think this is one of the hardest parts of losing a pet. When we lose a human loved one, our friends and family expect us to grieve for some time. However, a lot of people don't understand how much it can hurt to lose a pet. They don't realize that, often, the loss of a pet can leave a bigger hole in our lives

51

than human loss, because pets share such a big part of our daily lives.

I suggest you don't talk about your loss to people you know won't understand. Comments like, "After all it was just a cat, be thankful it wasn't one of your family!" do little to comfort you, belittle the relationship you had with your cat and may make you feel like you shouldn't grieve over the loss. Instead, talk about your loss to people you know will understand. It's important to have the chance to verbalize to someone understanding what you're feeling.

I suggest you let yourself feel all those feelings of hurt and emptiness. Don't suppress them, they won't go away until you really let yourself experience them. Think about your Abyssinian, look at pictures of her, let yourself cry. Those are your feelings and you own them. Feel them and experience them. It is only by going through this process that we can ever work through the grief. Many large cities have grief counseling groups available through animal medical centers or humane societies. If you live in or around a large city, you may want to see if such a group is available.

Q: *My fifteen-year-old kitty has become very sick after struggling for sometime against FIV. It's the hardest decision I've ever made, but I've decided it's time to put her to sleep. I want to be sure that it isn't going to be painful for her. Can you tell me how it's done?*

A: Bless your heart, I've been through this many times with my own pets as well as hundreds of times with client's pets. It is always hard. You can rest assured that euthanasia is not painful when done by a professional with the proper equipment and medications.

Most veterinarians use a simple overdose of a general anesthetic. It is injected slowly in the vein so that the pet simply goes to sleep, as if she were going into surgery. The overdose ensures she will drift into deep sleep, then slowly her heart and respiratory functions will stop. It is a very peaceful way to go.

I've seen hundreds of animals give a deep relaxing sigh during the procedure, as if to say, "Thank goodness, I don't have to struggle anymore, I'm free to move on."

Q: *I have made the decision that my terminally ill Siamese is in pain now and should be allowed to pass on. I don't want him to feel as though I've abandoned him, though. I'd like to stay with him while the veterinarian puts him down. Is that typically allowed and do you think that's a good idea?*

A: It is a difficult and painful decision to euthanize a pet. Some owners feel very strongly that they want to be there for their pet to the end. I understand and respect that feeling. If you feel that way, I think it is important for you to be there. I want your kitty to know you are there and you love him. It will make him more calm. I want the thoughts of the years of love and memories you two have shared to drift with him as he goes.

Discuss your wishes with your veterinarian. Some veterinarians either don't like for you to be in the room for this procedure, or simply won't allow it. I think this is because they feel it may be harder on you to witness the death, or because they are uncomfortable with the outpouring of emotions that naturally follow. If your veterinarian won't allow it, you may wish to find one who will. You should not be robbed of this important time by someone else's inability to handle it. I suggest you call first and see if your doctor will let you be there.

The doctor should counsel with you, answer all of your questions and give you plenty of time in a quiet room with him before it is done. Once the euthanasia is finished, the doctor should leave the room and let you have some quiet time with your cat. My thoughts are with you and I sympathize with your loss.

Q: *Our family has a wonderful Siamese who is eighteen years old. Cat Ballou has abdominal cancer which we have been helping her fight, but she seems to be getting weaker and weaker. I'm afraid the time is coming to make a really hard decision. How do we know when it's time?*

A: First of all, think about how lucky Cat Ballou is to have had such a nice long life with a family who loves her so much. You've obviously taken excellent care of her.

This is one of the most difficult decisions you will ever make in your life—and it's painful. My rule of thumb on deciding when it's time to put a beloved pet to sleep is to ask yourself this question: Is life fun for Cat Ballou anymore? I would say that if she can get up and down without too much pain, eat and eliminate without too much trouble, respond to your petting and be interactive, then she probably still enjoys being with you.

However, if she cannot exist within these necessary and dignified boundaries, life probably isn't fun for her anymore and the most humane thing you can do is let her go to sleep and be rid of the pain. If Cat Ballou seems to be in pain, has difficulty walking and appears to be in misery, then it is time.

Animals have a way of communicating this to us. Allow yourself to be open to her communications and you may be surprised at the feelings and insight you receive. If you decide it is time, remember this: Cat Ballou has given to you, unconditionally for eighteen years. Now you have a chance, one last time, to give to her some final peace and rest.

Q: *This is just the hardest thing for me. My twenty-two-year-old Persian is very sick, and I've made the decision to let her go on. I live in an apartment and don't have anywhere I can bury her. What will be done with her body and what options do I have?*

A: Most veterinary hospitals have made arrangements for either cremation at the hospital, or they may have an area pet cemetery pick up animals that die or are euthanized for proper burial. It is unfortunate that most city regulations won't allow burial of animals in household back yards, because that's where I'd like to have my pets. But it is an important law in place to protect human health. If you live in the country you can have your own pet cemetery area under a favorite tree—I like that idea.

If the hospital does not have such arrangements made, then I suggest you call ahead, today, and find a pet cemetery or crematorium. If you wait until Monday, your emotions will keep you from thinking clearly. Ask if the facility is a member of The Pet Loss Foundation or The International Association of Pet Cemeteries. IAPC is based in South Bend, Indiana, and can refer you to a reputable cemetery.

Q: *Three months ago I lost my wonderful Scottish Fold cat, Panda. I still hurt so bad over the loss and miss him terribly. My family tried to surprise me with a new kitten, but I just don't think I'm ready for another pet yet. I told them I'd know when I was ready. Don't you think that's true?*

A: Yes, I do. I think you're smart in taking your time to grieve over Panda. If you're not ready for another pet yet, it won't help to have a new kitten around. As a matter of fact, I've found people have difficulty bonding to a new pet if they haven't had adequate time to grieve over their loss. A lot of people feel pressured into accepting a new pet when well-meaning friends or family members try to "cheer them up" by trying to replace the lost pet. I think you are very smart to go with your gut feelings.

Thank your family, and explain to them that you will probably be ready for a new cat one day, but you're not prepared for that commitment right now.

Grief is a process that you must go through. There is no textbook time for recovery from a loss—human friend or pet companion. Each day that goes by the pain gets a little less and the emptiness subsides. That could be weeks, it could be months.

There will come a day when you'll decide you'd like to have another furry friend. Just remember, any new kitty will be very different than Panda, each personality unique. The new kitty won't replace Panda, no kitty could. Your next kitty will be wonderful in its own unique way, however, and you will develop a brand new relationship that will, in its own way be as special and as meaningful as the one you had with Panda. My condolences to you.

Q: *My husband and I recently lost our six-year-old Devon Rex. We have never been so attached to a pet, and the pain of loss is almost unbearable. I don't ever want another cat. I can't stand to think about going through this kind of pain again!*

A: I can really relate with that feeling! It does hurt bad, but that's good! It means you care and will allow yourself to truly enjoy animal companionship. Many people never allow themselves to experience the joy of human–pet bonding and the priceless enrichment of their lives pet animals can bring. They either were raised in a family that didn't have pets, or are truly afraid of "getting too close" and experiencing the hurt.

But you should know, after living with your Devon Rex, how valuable having a kitty around the house can be. Don't deny yourself that joy based on fresh pain. Give yourself a proper amount of time to heal. Be happy you and your husband had such a wonderful cat and take pride in the fact that he had you! Soon, you'll begin to miss the life a cat brings to the house, the constant, unconditional companionship a new pet pal will offer. Then and only then, why not head to your local humane society and save a life. That kitty you save will generate his own special place in your heart and his own special memories for you.

CHAPTER 7

Spaying and Neutering

"Doc, our cat, Bouncer, is always getting into fights. He spends most of his time outside, but he has lots of room in the back yard and he has his own toys and area where he sleeps. What can we do to keep him from getting into so many fights?"

"I would suggest you make Bouncer an indoor cat and have him neutered!"

"No way! I can't do that to him! He's been my pal for years."

Some men have a real problem with neutering their pets! It is a human psychological "thing," but it becomes an animal population "thing." Nonneutered pets also get into more fights and have more medical problems than their neutered counterparts.

The only people who should have intact cats are professional cat breeders. Breeding cats is a very specialized business and should be left up to the pros. Why do we think that if we have a dog or a cat we should automatically have a litter? If we had a horse do we automatically think of breeding it to get another horse? If you had a pet alligator, do you really want to breed it for more alligators? *Pets are not breeding machines.* There is no obligation attached to pet ownership that requires you to *make more!*

In my opinion, pets are to be enjoyed for what they offer *as individuals*, not for what their offspring potential is. Additionally, I can say with some authority that inexperienced people who try to have a litter are in for much more than they imagine. In almost every case you lose money, even if that was the primary reason for the breeding. Also, people far underestimate the time commitment required for a litter of puppies or kitties.

Q: We have a lovely cat named Celia. She is the most beautiful Siamese you've ever seen. We want to breed her because she is so great. We respect your opinion, what do you think?

A: I can understand this feeling. I have wonderful cats myself and I've often though how much I'd like one of their offspring. But if I had an offspring from all my favorite cats, not only would I be overrun with cats, but I would have been responsible for hundreds, even thousands, of cats that would not have been able to come home with me.

We forget that cats have many offspring in one litter, and these offspring go on to have other offspring and so on. In fact, one litter can turn into almost fourteen million cats in just ten years! When you look at it that way, it really opens your eyes.

I suggest this: each time you get a new pet, it is a new beginning. A totally new relationship is developed and each is special and will bring you great memories all of your life. I encourage you to develop the best relationship you can with Celia and love her for herself. Do this with every pet you have and I guarantee they will all be just as special, each in a different way.

Q: Our cat is acting very strange. She's only five months old and is meowing, yowling, not eating and acts like she is in pain. What's going on?

A: It sounds like your cat is in heat! Cats reach sexual maturity by five months of age. Cats are pretty persistent about being bred and make vocal and physical nuisances out of themselves until they are "satisfied." They come into heat in relationship to the diurnal cycle or season (lengthening of the daylight periods). Once they start coming into heat, they do so often, every two to three weeks, or until they are bred.

This adds an extra problem dogs do not have. This little trait is known as being seasonally polyestrus and occurs from about February through September. The only way to prevent this problem is to have her bred, or spayed. Of course, I recommend the latter. If you think she is behaving strangely now, wait until you see her go through a pregnancy and nursing a litter of kittens. Believe me, the spay operation is what she needs.

Q: *Is there a birth-control pill for cats?*

A: No. Unlike dogs, cats don't have the luxury of a birth-control pill. You either need to decide to have a pet, or a breeding animal. Unless you're in the business of breeding cats, I would recommend you not even think twice about breeding your cat.

Q: *Give me one good reason why we should castrate our cat!*

A: Here are four:

1. You will not be bothered by his constant meowing and yowling whenever a female cat is in heat anywhere within a five-mile radius.
2. You will not have your cat spraying very smelly urine around your house because that hormonal behavior is eliminated by neutering.
3. Your cat will be healthier for the rest of his life due to a decrease in hormone causes and behavioral causes for disease.
4. You will be doing your part for preventing pet overpopulation. *Every* pet makes a big difference. Fifteen million dogs and cats are put to death every year in our country because nonspayed and nonneutered dogs and cats are allowed to roam the streets and breed without restraint. That is a tragic statistic that you can help with. You are either part of the problem or part of the cure.

Q: *I just think a male cat needs to be a man, you know? Why are you so hot on this castration thing?*

A: Many men in our society have a real anxiety about castration. In fact, that is why, long ago we veterinarians began calling the procedure neutering! But even so, many men will not allow their male pets to be neutered for no other reason than their own fear of castration. They actually feel the fear, anxiety, pain and regret that would go along with such a thing in humans, when they think about neutering their male cat.

I'm no human psychologist, but I've certainly spoken with many of these men on my talk show. I can only make the case for all the good that neutering male pets does.

Q: *We used to neuter all the cats at my dad's barn by sticking their heads in a boot and just clipping them. It's really no big deal. They were just as good as mousers.*
A: Your point is well taken. It is not a difficult surgery, but I would never recommend anyone do it in quite that way. Pain is a real thing in pets, and our modern day anesthetics are inexpensive and safe. I would only want to see this done by a professional.

As far as behavior changes, I believe the only behavior changes that occur are for the better. Neutered males are more affectionate, they do not fight or roam indiscriminately, they do not succumb to many diseases their intact brothers do and they still chase mice in the barn just as well.

Q: *We missed the opportunity to spay our cat. She has come into heat for the second time. There are male cats everywhere now. How soon can we have her spayed?*
A: Good question. The uterus is inflamed and more vascular for several weeks after an estrus or heat cycle. I would recommend waiting two to three weeks after you know she is out of heat before spaying her. In the meantime, do your best to keep her in the house and don't let any of the males in. Use moth balls in coffee cans, a Scat Mat, or some commercial repelling chemical outdoors to keep the stray males away.

Q: *Our six-year-old cat is, unfortunately, pregnant. She's on a regular grocery-store food now and really doesn't look all that great. Should we change her diet to help her?*
A: I would get her on a higher-quality food immediately. I recommend Hill's Science Diet, Iams, Nature's Recipe or other high-quality, pet-store brands. They have the finest ingredients and are easily absorbable. I do not recommend supplementing her diet with vitamins or calcium unless your veterinarian specifically prescribes it. There may be other supplementation your veterinarian suggests after seeing her.

Ask your veterinarian about her vaccinations and deworming. It is too late to vaccinate her now, but she should be up-to-date to impart good immunity to the kittens. Most kitties get worms from their mother, both through the placenta and through the milk. Therefore, if she is worm free, you are less likely to be bothered with that problem.

Q: *Our cat was out all night and we fear she has been bred by a neighborhood stray. Can we get her a shot or something to abort this pregnancy?*

A: Yes, the so called "mismating" shot can be given in cats if within thirty-six to forty-eight hours after the breeding. It is a drug called ECP and is not without complication. It is a large dose of female hormone and makes the uterus not receptive to implantation by the fertilized ova. You must be aware of the potential risk. Uterine problems or anemia may occur secondary to the injection, although these are not as common in the cat as they are in dogs who receive this mismating shot.

May I suggest you get your cat spayed and then turn her into an indoor cat. She will live longer!

Q: *We were going to spay our four-year-old house cat, but in the meantime, she got pregnant. We do not want her to have a litter. Can we go ahead and spay her now?*

A: If she is in her first trimester of pregnancy, you can spay her while she is pregnant. Remember, anytime you do this, the surgery is more complicated and carries with it a higher risk The uterus is active, vascular and more likely to bleed. There is more fluid loss and a larger change to her hormone cycles. But it is a relatively safe procedure and is recommended especially in a case like yours.

PART II

GENERAL CARE
AND GROOMING

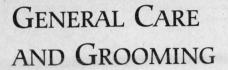

CHAPTER 8

Bathing, Grooming and Shedding

"Doc, I need some serious help. My wife has been away for a few weeks and she is real concerned that I take good care of her cat, Roger. Believe me, my life depends on this. The problem is she is coming home tomorrow and I have to bathe this cat. I've never done that before in my life."

"Why do you have to bathe Roger?"

"Well, he was out in the garage when I was working on my car and I kinda spilled some oil on him."

It is a common misconception that cats never need baths since they groom themselves so frequently. It is true that some cats are thorough groomers who will need only the occasional bath. Other cats, however, really groom only superficially and need routine baths to help them stay clean and healthy. In parts of the country where fleas are a problem, cats may need a bath every week during flea season.

I receive a good number of questions on talk radio not only about when and how often to bathe cats, but *how* to bathe cats. I'll admit that it can be an exhausting and somewhat dangerous task for the inexperienced and poorly prepared. However, with good planning and patience, cat bathing doesn't have to be traumatic for either you or your cat.

Another subject which generates a lot of calls is shedding. All cats shed. Seasonal shedding occurs in the spring and fall, the normal cycle of haircoat turnover. Nonseasonal shedding occurs at all other times and is lighter but constant. There are factors that can either increase or decrease shedding, and there are ways that we, as cat owners, can minimize excess hair on our furniture and clothes.

Q: *I always thought cats cleaned themselves with their tongues and didn't need baths, but my kitty's fur seems to get oily and stand up in clumps. Could he need a bath? How often should I bathe him?*

A: Yes, if his fur is looking oily and separating into clumps, he probably does need a bath. How often to bathe a cat must be decided on an individual basis for each cat. Some cats will rarely ever require a bath. This is especially true for some shorthaired cats who are fastidious groomers, live indoors and never have a problem with fleas. Other cats may need a bath as often as once a week if they suffer from a skin allergy or have a continuous exposure to fleas. Most longhaired cats require some help with grooming by having a routine bath and regular brushing.

   If your cat doesn't seem to need a bath, then don't bathe him on a regular basis just to be doing it. Regular brushing is more important to the health of your cat's skin and haircoat. Too much bathing can rob the coat of natural oils and moisture. While it may be necessary to bathe regularly, to control fleas, for example, don't overdo it. Do bathe him often enough for him to get used to baths being part of his routine. The hardest cats to bathe are the ones who are bathed rarely. A gentle bath every three to four months will keep him tolerating baths without too much retraining.

Q: *Dr. Jim, at what age is it best to start bathing a cat?*

A: It's best to establish bathing as part of a cat's routine early in its life. This is true of grooming in general. If a kitten gets used to being brushed, having its nails trimmed and being bathed while it is young, it learns to trust being handled by you and takes these things in stride as part of its routine.

   I would recommend starting to get a kitten used to bathing by the time it is twelve to sixteen weeks old. Don't overdo bathing, but bathe your kitty often enough to establish it as a routine part of its grooming, once every three or four months. Cats who are rarely bathed usually resist badly.

Q: *I need to bathe my cat because he really has a bad flea problem. When I tried to bathe him though, he climbed right up me. I had scratches all over my arms and my face, not to mention having to chase my sudsy cat all through the house and drag him hissing and spitting back to the bathtub. I must be doing something wrong. How do I keep him under control?*

A: Bathing an adult cat, who has not been bathed much, can be very tricky. If you're not careful, you can get seriously scratched or bitten. To add to the problem, your cat has had at least one bad experience with bathing.

There are a couple of key points to making bathing a cat safer and easier:

1. Prepare carefully before you ever start.
2. Have someone help you if your cat doesn't behave well while being bathed.

Try to close off the area where you bathe your cat, so that if he escapes, he can't take off through the house and end up under the bed.

Make sure you have a safe, nonslip surface for the cat to stand on in the sink or bathtub. A regular window screen with a metal frame works well, or a stiff plastic screen. This gives kitty something to sink his claws into (other than you) while letting the water drain through. If you use a bathtub to bathe your cat, tip the screen at an angle toward the back of the tub (away from you) so that he climbs up and away from you if he gets panicked.

Have someone help you hold kitty. Take your time, stay patient, and expect to get wet. Don't lose your temper or get angry if he panics and tries to climb up you. Getting angry or punishing kitty will only make him more scared. Stay calm and talk to him in a sympathetic and loving voice.

Hold kitty in the sink by holding gentle pressure with one hand on his shoulders and one hand in front of his chest. If he starts to panic, stop what you're doing and hold him down in the sink by the scruff of his neck until he calms down. (Don't pick him up by the scruff of his neck—this can injure an adult cat—just hold him down in the sink.) Once he calms down, you can start again. Keep talking to him in a calm, sympathetic voice, and take your time.

If at any time, he really panics badly and you can't control him, toss a large towel over him and scoop him up so that only his head is out of the towel. Slip him into his cat carrier and let him sit in there until he calms down. Don't get mad at him. Patience is vital. Once he calms down, you can continue.

Q: *I have never bathed a cat before. How exactly should I do it?*
A: First decide where you are going to give the bath. You can use the bathtub, the bathroom sink or the kitchen sink. I like using the kitchen sink best because there is already a spray attachment there and I can stand and don't have to lean over. The downside to most kitchens is that it's hard to close off the area in case of an escape. If your cat escapes it's liable to run through the house and under the bed. Wherever you decide to give the bath, you will need a spray attachment for the faucet.

Next, assemble all the supplies you will use before you ever go get kitty.

You will need:
- metal or stiff plastic screen for the cat to stand on
- mineral oil or eye ointment
- cotton balls
- two washcloths
- several large towels
- cat-safe shampoo
- plastic squeeze bottle (if the shampoo is not already in one)
- coat conditioner (if needed)
- nail clippers
- cat brush
- cat carrier

Clear everything else out of the way of the sink area, especially anything breakable. Place the screen in the bottom of the sink before you go get your cat.

First trim kitty's claws to minimize the chance of injury to you should he get panicked. Next, gently brush your cat to remove as much loose and dead hair as possible. While you're doing this, talk to your kitty in a soothing, loving way to relax him.

Put a few drops of eye ointment or mineral oil in each eye and place a cotton ball in each ear. Place the cat gently in the sink and hold him there lightly by putting one hand on top of his shoulders. Use as little resistance as possible, but be prepared to grab him if he tries to jump. This takes a little practice, so use an assistant to help hold kitty if he's really resistant.

Turn the water on slowly and let it run until it is warm, *not hot*. Turn the water on very low, so the spray is not hard. Hold the sprayer right up against kitty's skin so the spray won't scare him. Your assistant can hold up his front legs for you to wet the fur on his stomach and between his legs. Once he is wet, turn off the water and start to lather him. It helps to dilute the shampoo with warm water prior to starting. It makes the shampoo lather easier and rinse more cleanly. Start lathering at his neck and work back toward the tail. Lather the tail, legs, feet and belly well. Then take your washcloth and wash his face. Rinse carefully. Be sure to remove all traces of shampoo. Any residue could cause irritation and itching. If he's especially dirty, you may want to lather again. Follow up with coat conditioner on the back, belly and tail, if desired. Rinse very well again. Run your hand through the coat. It should feel squeaky clean and not slick or slippery. Continue to rinse until all areas feel clean.

After rinsing, run your hands down kitty's back, legs and tail to remove excess water. Take a large towel and place it over kitty and scoop him up so that only his head is out of the towel. Put him on the cabinet and gently towel his body, legs and tail. Replace the towel with a dry one and towel him off again. If you like, you can switch to a dry towel again and wrap kitty up like a burrito and hold him a while until he warms up. My cats seem to like that and will sit very contented for a good thirty minutes while being held this way. When I unwrap them, they're well on their way to being dry.

Q: Can I use my blow dryer to dry my cat after I bathe her?

A: Some cats will tolerate the use of a blow dryer if you introduce them to it very slowly and very carefully. Be sure to use only low to medium settings of cool or medium heat, *never high or hot settings*. Don't point the air straight at the cat's face at any time. Be sure to hold the dryer at least one foot away at all times.

When the cat is mostly dry, you can start to brush her as you blow the hair. Don't try to brush her while she's still wet as that can tangle and damage the hair and harm the skin.

Q: I've heard it's dangerous to use dog shampoos on cats. Is that true? What is the best type of shampoo for cats?

A: You do have to be more careful in selecting a shampoo for cats than for dogs. This is especially true for medicated shampoos and flea shampoos. The concentration of medication or insecticide in dog shampoos may be too strong for cats and can cause illness or even death. It is very important to read the label carefully. Use only shampoos that are labeled to be safe for cats. Be extra careful when purchasing flea dip. Make sure it says on the label that it is approved safe for use on cats.

If your cat has a skin allergy, your veterinarian may prescribe a medicated shampoo. Skin allergies are less common in cats than in dogs, so many medicated shampoos are formulated for dogs only. Read the label and make sure it states that the shampoo is safe for cats.

Do not use household products such as dishwashing detergents to wash your cat. These products contain harsh detergents that can irritate the skin and strip the coat of natural oils. They may also leave an irritating residue which can result in scratching and encourage infections.

Q: I've heard you say to be careful about a cat's eyes and ears when you bathe it. What precautions should I take?

A: Use a little eye ointment or mineral oil in each eye before you begin. This helps prevent any chemical irritation should shampoo get near your cat's eyes. Also, put a cotton ball in each ear to prevent water from getting into the ear canal. Water accumulation may spark irritation or an infection.

When you bathe your cat, don't spray water directly on her face. Use a washcloth and gently wet the face. Then take a very small amount of shampoo on the washcloth and wash the face, staying away from the area around the eyes. Wet a cotton ball with clean water to gently wipe around the eye area. Once you've lathered the rest of the head, take a clean washcloth wet with clean water and gently scrub the face to remove all lather. Don't forget to remove the cotton from her ears when you're done!

Q: *Is it OK to use flea shampoo on my new kitten? She's six weeks old.*

A: You'll need to read the label on the shampoo and see if it's approved for use on young kittens. Most flea shampoos are not, although there are some that are, as well as some mild flea soaps that can be used on kittens.

Unless your new kitten has a severe flea infestation, I'd prefer you simply use a regular shampoo which is approved for kittens. I like to keep chemicals away from young animals as much as possible. The bath itself will probably drown most of the fleas.

Q: *My cat sheds constantly. She also scratches a lot and seems to have dandruff type flakes. She is a mixed-breed longhair. Do you think vitamins would help?*

A: Shedding can be increased by allergies, disease and low levels of skin inflammation from various causes. The first thing I suggest is to make sure you are feeding your cat a high quality cat food. One of the premium brands available from a pet store or your veterinary clinic will provide your cat with the best quality nutrition. The healthier your cat's skin and coat are, the less she'll shed. Vitamin supplements are not necessary if your cat is on a premium food. You can overdo vitamins.

As cat owners, we can decrease the amount of hair that ends up in our house and on our clothes by regular brushing and occasional bathing of our cats. Regular grooming removes the dead hair from the coat. This helps prevent matting of the dead hair and helps prevent hairballs from the cat swallowing dead hair as he grooms himself. You may also want to try a "stop-shed" type spray to decrease her nonseasonal shedding.

Q: *I have a four-year-old Himalayan. She has problems with mats in her "armpits" and on her belly. She has also been scratching a lot. Why does she get these mats? Is that why she's scratching?*

A: Your cat could be scratching for a number of reasons: fleas, dry skin, insect bites or irritation from dirty skin. She could also be scratching just due to the irritation of the mats. To prevent these mats from forming, you'll need to do a better job of grooming her regularly.

Longhaired cats require regular brushing to remove dead hair. If, as she sheds, the dead hair is not removed, it will form mats. She will scratch in an attempt to remove the dead hair. This scratching not only irritates the skin, but makes the mats worse. Irritated skin becomes inflamed and this causes it to ooze more oils. These excess oils on the skin are the perfect place for bacteria to grow. This bacterial growth causes a secondary bacterial skin infection and the spot gets worse. As you can see, this can become a vicious cycle very quickly.

Mats that are not taken care of promptly can become very bad and may require your cat being shaved by a professional groomer to solve the problem. Your cat depends on you to keep her healthy and comfortable by grooming her regularly. It's one of the responsibilities you take on when you get a cat. Obviously, longhaired cats and those with thick haircoats require more grooming than shorthaired breeds.

You should thoroughly brush your cat each week, making sure all mats are carefully worked out. A quicker, daily brushing in between makes this job easier and keeps more hair off your furniture and floor.

Q: *How often is it necessary to groom shorthaired cats? We have two Siamese who live indoors all the time.*

A: Shorthaired breeds such as your Siamese obviously don't require the amount of grooming that longhaired, thick-coated breeds such as a Persian would. However, shorthaired cats also need brushing. Their coats shed out as well, and a good brushing removes dead hair and stimulates the skin's natural oils.

Regular grooming also gives you a chance to check your cat over on a regular basis and look for health problems. While grooming, you should feel for any lumps or bumps. Early detection of cysts or tumors gives your cat a better chance to recover from these. Minor injuries such as cuts, insect bites and abrasions can be hidden under a cat's coat, but you'll be sure to find them with a thorough grooming.

Q: *We have a beautiful silver Persian. In the summer, I find it very difficult to keep him well treated for fleas with his thick, long coat. Not to mention he sheds something terrific every spring. Is it possible to shave a cat for the spring and summer?"*

A: Actually, yes it is. I wouldn't recommend trying to do it yourself though. It's not an easy job to shave a cat. A professional cat groomer can shave your Persian in a short summer cut, sometimes called a "lion cut." It's called this because the hair is left natural on the head and neck and a tuft of hair is typically left on the end of the tail, resulting in your kitty looking like a little lion.

It certainly decreases the amount of time necessary for grooming a Persian during the summer, as well as decreasing the amount of hair shed in your home. The other benefit is that it makes it much simpler for products such as flea sprays to reach the skin.

If you decide to do this, wait until the warm weather has stabilized or better yet, keep your kitty indoors. Enough hair should be left to give your kitty's skin all the protection from sun, temperature and environment that a shorthaired cat would have.

Q: *Is there a way to speed up the spring shedding process? It seems to take my cat forever to shed out her winter coat.*

A: You'll need to help this process by daily brushing during this shedding season. With longhaired cats, a fine-toothed comb is the best way to remove dead hairs from the heavy undercoat. Shorthaired cats do well with rubber curry brushes and hand rubbing. A couple of good baths will also speed the removal of dead and loose hair.

Removing the dead, loose hair also helps provide your cat with insulation against summer heat. A well-brushed haircoat enables air to circulate between the hairs and down to the skin, increasing the cat's natural cooling mechanisms and making him more comfortable in hot weather.

Q: *What's the best way to remove mats? I have a longhaired mixed-breed cat who gets a thick coat during the winter. In the spring, he always ends up with bad mats on his hindquarters, belly and behind his front legs.*

A: Spring is one of the worst times for longhaired cats to get mats because they are shedding the downy undercoat hairs that give the coat insulation in the winter. If the dead hairs aren't removed by grooming, they can easily mat. The best way to prevent bad mats from forming is to comb and brush your cat daily during this high shedding season.

Try to untangle the mats first using your fingers. Be careful not to pull on the sensitive skin as you untangle the hair. With one hand, hold the hair just above the skin while you untangle with the other hand. Let the pull be on your fingers, not on the skin. It's easy to hurt a cat's sensitive skin while trying to remove mats. If you hurt him, he'll lose trust in you and start to dislike grooming. You want grooming to be a positive bond between you and him.

Get as much of the mat out as you can with your fingers, and then use a grooming comb that has widely spaced teeth on one end and closely spaced teeth on the other. Start with the wide end and when it goes through the hair easily, use the fine end. (Every longhaired cat owner should invest in this type of comb.) Continue to hold the hair close to the skin with one hand so that the skin isn't pulled every time you pull the comb through the hair.

If the mat is really tough, you can try putting a few drops of mineral oil on the mat and trying to untangle it gently with the comb or your fingers. *Don't wet the mat or wash a cat with mats, as that will set the mat in permanently and you will have no choice but to cut it out.*

There are some helpful grooming tools, called mat rakes, which will cut through mats without injuring the cat's skin. They are available at pet shops and sometimes at veterinary clinics.

If none of this works, the mats will have to be cut out or the cat clipped. I recommend you let a professional groomer do this for you. Cat's skin is very loose and it is very difficult sometimes to distinguish where the mat ends and the skin begins. I have sewed up bad cuts in a lot of cats whose owners attempted to cut out mats and cut skin instead.

The best way to avoid all this headache is to not ignore grooming until mats get this bad.

CHAPTER 9

Nails, Ears, Eyes and Dental Health

"We have tried to get rid of ear mites for months now. Nothing we've tried works."

"How have you treated your cat?"

"We have used everything the vet gave us. Now my neighbor says we should be using some kind of special oil from the health food store."

"No, I mean how have you treated the cat, on what schedule?"

"We just treat every day and we've used everything you can imagine. I just don't know what to do with this cat. . . ."

"OK, take a deep breath! How you treat is more important than what you treat with. You must use an appropriate medicine and then treat for seven days, wait about a week, then treat all over again for seven full days. This gets all of the life stages of the mite."

"I heard there was some new oil with ozone in it. Can I use that?"

Most cat owners don't pay much attention to their cats' ears. Although they are a small part of the cat's body, they can cause some big health problems if neglected. In fact, ear problems are responsible for a large number of cats' visits to their veterinarians. Regular checks of your cat's ears and periodic cleaning will help keep him healthy. It will also allow you to spot problems early and get your kitty to the veterinarian before a small problem becomes a big one.

A cat's mouth is probably the most overlooked and neglected part of a cat's body. According to veterinary dental specialists, 85% of all cats over four years old suffer from dental problems.

Periodontal disease is the most common dental problem in cats. It can start very early in a cat's life, resulting in the loss of teeth by the time a cat is two years old. Cats may also suffer from cavities.

Cats have a highly developed sense of vision. They rely more on their sense of sight than they do on their sense of smell. The eye is a very delicate organ and when injured or otherwise affected needs immediate care.

Finally the claws. It is very helpful to keep the claws trimmed down to a blunt point to decrease the need to scratch and decrease the damage done by scratching.

Q: *Our white Persian has rust-colored stains at the corners of her eyes. What causes this? Is there anyway to get rid of the stains?*

A: These are tear stains, which are common in white cats. They result from the pH level of the tears, which evaporate. There are several brands of tear-stain removers available through pet shops and groomers which will lighten these stains. In addition, if the tearing is excessive, your veterinarian can prescribe antibiotic eye drops which can decrease the amount of tearing. Some tearing will always occur however.

Q: *Dr. Jim, my three-year-old Burmese, Hershey, is very good about using his scratching post. He never has scratched on the furniture, but sometimes when he is sitting on my lap he'll take off real fast and will scratch me with his back claws. He has also caused snags on my clothes that way. Is there anything I can do to prevent this?*

A: Most cats are very good about keeping their claws retracted when they're not using them, but at times, like when they push off in a hurry, the claws may accidentally catch you.

The best prevention is to keep Hershey's claws trimmed about every ten to fourteen days. The front claws tend to grow faster than the back claws and may need trimming more often. Once the sharp point of the claw is removed, the blunt claw remaining will have much less tendency to scratch or snag clothing. You can also smooth the blunt end of the claw after trimming by using a nail file or emery board. This will help even more.

Q: *Dr. Jim, I've heard you talk about trimming cats' claws. Can you tell me how to do this at home?*

A: Trimming your cat's claws is really very easy once you and your cat get used to it. The key is to take your time and have patience.

It helps to pick a time when your cat isn't feeling especially active, perhaps after a meal when he's feeling kind of sleepy. It might help to have someone help you at first. Simply push on the cat's toe using your thumb and forefinger to make the claw extend. Then trim, using claw trimmers from a pet store, or sharp human nail trimmers. Cut only the white part of the claw. If you cut into the pink part of the claw, you may make the nail bleed and cause the cat pain.

If your cat will not let you do all four paws at one time, simply do one paw at a time until he doesn't mind having them all done at once. I would do this every week or two to keep the claws blunt. If let go, cats' claws can get long and sharp like a hawk's talons.

Q: *Our cat has come home after being gone for about two weeks. He has a swollen right ear. What do you think might have happened?*

A: I'll bet your cat is an intact male and has been out "catting" around. Intact males get into a lot of fights. In addition to bite wounds and abscesses, one common injury is an aural hematoma. A blood pocket forms inside the ear flap because of trauma, either a bite or a sharp claw scratch. This causes bleeding inside the two layers of skin that make up the ear flap. The blood has nowhere to go and fills the ear flap like a fluid sac.

Your veterinarian will need to see this cat. These cases usually require a minor surgery to relieve the blood pressure and help restore the ear flap to normal anatomy.

Q: *Our cat is being treated for ear mites. Our vet told us to be sure to bathe the cat once a week for three weeks. Why is that?*

A: The little bug that causes ear-mite infestations is akin to the spider. This means there are adult mites and young ones, too. The young ones are more resistant to treatment than the adults, and that is why you must treat for seven days, wait a week for the young ones to mature into adults, then treat again for seven days.

Some of the immature stages of the mite can be dislodged onto the cat's paws and rear legs because of the scratching, then can reinfest the cat after treatment in the ear is completed. Therefore it is best to bathe the cat a couple of times during the treatment of ear mites to help get rid of any immature stages on the fur coat.

Q: *Our cat, Macho, came home from a few days out and had an obvious injury to his right eye. It seems to be getting worse. Should we take him to the vet?*

A: Absolutely! The eye is a very delicate structure and an injury can cause sometimes irreversible damage if let go just a few hours too long.

A simple scratch on the cornea can turn into an infection that can cause the cat to lose the eye. I've seen cat fight wounds cause a puncture to the cornea and allow parts of the iris to protrude through the puncture. If this is not treated immediately, there will be permanent damage, possible loss of eyesight and potential loss of the eye.

There is not much you can do for eye injuries at home. A veterinarian must examine the eye and instigate proper treatment—and soon. Because the tissues are so delicate, even hours may be too long to wait.

Q: *My veterinarian says my cat has a cavity in an important tooth and should have a root canal! She has referred me to a veterinary dental specialist. Is this necessary?*

A: Yes, this is important for the health and well-being of your feline friend. Your cat's teeth are vital to its health. If a cat's mouth is painful, it cannot eat properly and its health will be jeopardized.

Cavities, although rare, occur in cats just as they do in people. If a cavity affects only the surface of a tooth and does not extend into the root system, it can be filled with a human dental filler called glass ionomer. This seals the cavity and releases fluoride ions which help decrease pain and slow bacterial growth.

If a cavity has moved into the root system of one of the smaller incisors or premolars, then the tooth is usually extracted. If, however, the cavity has affected the root system of one of the large important teeth such as the canines or the large premolars, then it should be saved if at all possible. This is done by performing a root canal, where the nerve of the tooth is removed along with the inflamed tissue surrounding it. Following this removal, the canal is filled, cleaned and dried. The tooth is then sealed at both ends to stop pain and prevent infection.

While most veterinarians are capable of extracting teeth, root canals are specialized procedures that should be performed by a veterinarian who is a dental specialist, if at all possible. Your veterinarian is right on target with her recommendations.

Q: *How can I prevent constant tartar on my cat's teeth?*
A: The best way to prevent tartar and periodontal disease is to have your veterinarian perform a thorough cleaning of your cat's teeth every year and then follow up at home by regularly brushing your cat's teeth. Your veterinarian can sell you a special toothbrush made especially for cats.

Make it part of your regular routine to open your cat's mouth and inspect the teeth and gums. Take a Q-tip and touch it gently to the gum line of each tooth. If there are any areas that are sensitive or bleeding, take your cat in to the veterinarian and let him check it out. Tartar and cavities can commonly occur just below the gum line where the tooth's enamel ends. Problems that are caught early may involve only the surface of the tooth and be easy to correct.

Also be alert to unusual bad breath when you check your cat's mouth. While most cats don't have great breath, a foul smell to the breath is indicative of an underlying problem, perhaps severe, with the teeth, gums or organ systems.

Feeding dry cat food, rather than only canned food, will also help your cat remove some tartar through chewing.

Q: Our veterinarian has suggested our six-year-old Siamese, Twiggy, have a dental prophy done. Do you think this is necessary?

A: Absolutely! Your vet is trying to save you some money and heartache. A dental prophy for your cat is just as important as it is for you. Because the teeth are not seen as regularly and, therefore, aren't treated as regularly, the gums can become inflamed and infected due to the constant buildup of tartar. Remember, the tartar buildup is considered normal, but it creates some abnormal consequences: inflamed, swollen gums and secondary infection that can sometimes become so severe as to cause a blood-borne infection that can settle in the kidneys!

Consequently, your vet should tranquilize Twiggy and scale or scrape the surfaces of the teeth to remove the tartar. Then the doctor will flush the gums, treat them if necessary, and you'll have a cat with a clean set of teeth. However, they will only stay that way if you take on the responsibility of brushing them yourself.

Q: After the veterinarian cleaned my cat's teeth, he sent me home with a special toothbrush and toothpaste. Exactly how do I brush my cat's teeth, and how often?

A: A young cat, one to three years, needs its teeth brushed about every week. Older than that, and it should go up to about three times a week. Senior cats probably need it five times a week.

Start slowly. Don't expect your cat to take to this idea right away. Wait about one week after dental cleaning to start so that his gums won't be sore. Pick a quiet, confined area where you can have good control of your cat. Be sure to use a toothbrush made especially for pets; they are much softer than a baby toothbrush. Also use only an enzyme toothpaste made for pets. Both the toothbrush and toothpaste are available through your veterinarian or pet shop.

Dip the end of the toothbrush in a little tuna juice and slide it gently into the corner of your cat's mouth, stroking along the teeth and then back out. Train your cat to accept this brushing in stages. Start with just a few seconds at a time.

Next time put a little toothpaste on the brush and dip both brush and paste in a little tuna juice. Slowly you can introduce the toothbrush and brush gently for a few seconds. Eventually you'll work up to a few minutes.

Remember, with pet toothpaste the enzyme action does the work, not the detergent or scrubbing action as with human toothpaste. Therefore it's more important to get the toothpaste in every crack and crevice than to scrub it around. Luckily, there is no need to rinse.

Q: *I think my four-year-old Himalayan, Lily, broke a tooth. She doesn't seem to feel well and isn't eating. She is also salivating a lot. What do I need to do?*

A: You'll need to get Lily to her veterinarian for immediate treatment. Broken teeth do occur in cats, especially those who like to chew on hard objects. Just as with people, a cat's broken tooth with its exposed nerve can be very painful. It often causes enough pain to make the cat unable to eat and overall very depressed.

A broken tooth detected early may be repaired. Once the tooth has abscessed, it will require extraction by a veterinarian. If not removed, the abscess could spread infection, via the bloodstream, through the body. Broken teeth always need veterinary care.

CHAPTER 10

Itching, Allergies and Skin Disease

"We were at the vet's this morning with our cat Jason. He's had this redness on his chin for about three weeks. The vet said it was acne! He prescribed scrubs and ointment. It cost $82! I told my wife to just stop by the drug store on the way home and buy some Clearasil and stop feeding him chocolate!"

Scratching pets are the number one medical reason people visit a veterinary hospital nationwide. Fleas account for over 50% of all such dermatological cases and over 35% of all veterinary work performed.

Ear mites are also a common problem that causes itching in cats, along with food allergies, inhaled allergies and contact allergies.

Cats have a whole array of skin diseases other than allergies. They suffer from various forms of skin cancer, fungal infections, hormone-related hair loss and many diseases for which we do not know the cause. Treatments are many times more effective if the disease is caught early and proper diagnosis and treatment are obtained.

Q: *Our cat, Sammy, has a crusty line of spots going up his back. We've treated it with ointment for several months but it just won't go away. Got any tips?*

A: Yes! Get to the vet's office and get that cat treated for fleas! It is a very common sign to have this "racing stripe" run up a cat's back when they are seriously affected by fleas. It is an area of crusty inflammation and hair loss due to the intense itching. Many times fleas are hard to see, and many people simply don't know what to look for. Therefore, some cats go untreated too long and can even have a secondary anemia due to the blood loss from a severe flea infestation.

The sign you describe usually occurs in severe flea-infestation cases, so I want you to get to a veterinarian right away. A cat can be anemic yet look normal to the casual observer. The fact that you have been treating these spots for months tells me your cat has been under flea attack for some time.

While your cat is at the animal hospital, review the four-step process to flea control (Chapter 14) and discuss on-pet flea control measures with the doctor. Good luck!

Q: *Our cat scratches every day. Because he is black and longhaired, we groom him often. We have seen only a flea or two all year, so we can't believe fleas are causing his itching. Any ideas?*

A: Because your cat is black and longhaired, it doesn't surprise me you see very few fleas. The fact that you have seen a few, indicates there are probably many.

To determine if your cat does have fleas, try putting the cat on a white surface, like butcher paper, then brush him. You will probably see small, black pepperlike dots come off during this combing. This is flea excrement, sometimes politely called "flea dirt." It is a positive sign of fleas. During a bath this flea dirt dissolves and turns bath water into a rusty color, also a positive sign of fleas. This color change is due to the dissolving of the blood contained in the excrement.

Q: *We've followed your advice for flea control, but Patches is still scratching. What else can we do?*

A: First of all don't give up on your flea-control program. Keep it up. For the itching it is sometimes necessary to resort to glucocorticoids to help cats get through a very intense flea season—even with expert flea-control measures.

Some cats will itch for months after even one flea bite. These cats should be put on oral steroids. Most veterinarians will agree with an every-other-day schedule of oral steroid after an initial loading dose every day for about a week.

Q: *Our little white cat has developed spots all over her face. She itches terribly and looks really bad. The vet has tested her for many different things, but thinks it's food allergy. He's put her on a homemade diet of lamb baby food and rice. Does this sound reasonable?*

A: Yes. Your veterinarian is to be commended for staying current. Food allergy used to be thought of as very rare. However, we are seeing more and more of it, and I am happy to hear your doctor is testing for it so soon.

Itching is the most common sign with food allergy. It can manifest in various ways but usually through crusty sores in various spots on the body. The head and neck seem quite common. If you have fed this test diet for three months and the symptoms begin to subside, then you have made a diagnosis of food allergy and you have essentially solved a serious problem.

Q: *Our veterinarian has put my cat on a test diet for allergies. He said she had to be on the diet for ten weeks. It is just lamb baby food. I know cats need taurine. Shouldn't I be adding taurine to the baby food?*

A: Good question. You've been reading! However in this case, because the ten to twelve weeks she will be on this test diet is a relatively short time, you do not need to supplement with taurine. Taurine deficiencies occur during long-term shortages in the diet. Three months without taurine will not hurt her. Once she is placed on a maintenance diet, be sure that it is taurine fortified.

Q: *Our wonderful cat, Jake, sits all day and licks his sides. Now he has his sides completely bald. That's more than just normal grooming, isn't it?*

A: I'd say yes. Jake may very well have atopy. Atopy is a term we use for a hereditary hypersensitivity causing an antigen–antibody reaction in the cat's body when exposed to an allergen. The number one sign is itching, but it may also be general scratching or excessive grooming. Sometimes cats will pull out hair in clumps, and some work particularly at their sides—like Jake.

I would take Jake to the doctor and ask about allergy testing him. The doctor will test for many different allergens by giving small injections under his skin. By judging the size of the skin reaction, the doctor can determine what Jake is allergic to.

To treat the allergy it is necessary to avoid the offending substance as much as you can. However, some offending substances, house dust for example, are almost impossible to avoid. In these cases, many veterinarians give corticosteriods to the cat to relieve the itching. Corticosteriods can be used for several months out of the year if the allergen is seasonal.

If the allergen is always present, a process called hyposensitization is done. The cat is actually given small doses of the allergen in an attempt to build up an immunity to the offending substance.

I have had good success in supplementing these cats with Omega 3 fatty acid supplements. These oils are not only good for the hair coat, but also have an anti-itching effect on cases like this. Some people have been able to use these supplements and either decrease or even eliminate steroid use.

Q: *Our eleven-year-old cat, Snowball, has had crusty spots on the edges of his ears for about eight months. He hates it when we try to peal the crusts off. The spots never heal and appear to be spreading. What could this be?*

A: I gather that Snowball is a white cat. White cats that have access to outdoors are more commonly affected by skin cancer. The symptoms you describe are typical for a form of skin cancer called squamous cell carcinoma. To be even more specific, it is probably Bowen's disease, a form of this cancer seen on the face, ears and neck of affected cats.

Treatment with conventional drugs is not very effective. If it is Bowen's disease, Snowball will need to undergo radiation therapy which is quite effective. It allows the spots to heal within two months and the cat can live a normal life after treatment.

You need to see a veterinarian who can properly diagnose and treat this type of skin cancer. Call around and tell the doctor we talked and see who seems most confident in handling the case. Good luck.

Q: *Our cat's face has looked funny for several weeks. Upon getting a good look, we discovered his lip was very swollen and raw looking. Has he gotten into some poison?*

A: That is a possibility, but so are many things with the symptoms you describe. He could have been stung by a venomous insect, cut in a fight, suffered a chemical burn and so on. You will need to take him to an animal hospital and have a complete examination done. A part of this examination will be a blood profile.

There is a condition called eosinophilic ulcer or rodent ulcer that looks like what you are describing. This is diagnosed by the classic type of sores found and a high blood eosinophil count. The cause of this problem is unknown. Researchers suspect mosquito bite hypersensitivity, inhaled allergies, food allergies, viral infections and feline leukemia.

The treatment for this strange disease involves the use of steroids and antibiotics. Many times veterinarians are able to get complete remission of the problem. Other more stubborn cases are treated with hypoallergenic foods, radio therapy, laser therapy and some even more exotic treatments.

Have your veterinarian make a diagnosis and then approach treatment carefully, from the most conservative approach first. You may get lucky and solve the problem immediately.

Q: *Our Siamese, Chin, has become neurotic since we brought home a new little puppy. We've tried to share our attention between the two, but puppies take more time. Now Chin has started losing his hair. Do you think the puppy has brought in fleas or something?*

A: There is a skin disease called psychogenic alopecia. In these cases the cat starts to pull out its hair as a way of relieving anxiety over something stressful in its environment. This is seen more commonly in the "high-strung" purebred cats like the Siamese, Burmese, Abyssinian and Himalayans.

The addition of a puppy to your household could most definitely cause stress for Chin, both because of the change in his environment and because of the competition for your attention. Considering these factors, I would venture to guess that Chin is suffering from psychogenic alopecia.

Treatment is essentially psychological. I would suggest you make a concerted effort to give Chin a great deal of private quality time several times a day. Make it clear to him that you have not abandoned him over the new puppy. Also make sure Chin has an area where he can get away from the puppy and be alone whenever he wants.

If this does stop the hair loss, you may try relaxing Chin by using phenobarb or Valium (given by your veterinarian). These drugs can modify Chin's mood and relieve some of the stress during this transition stage.

If the hair still does not start growing back in, you may have to use a restrictive Elizabethan collar to prevent the cat from reaching its belly and flanks with its mouth. If that does not cause the hair to return, then you are probably dealing with some other form of disease.

Q: *Our vet says our cat has acne. That sounds funny. Have you ever heard of acne in cats?*

A: Yes, it is actually quite common. It is caused by the same sort of process as we see in human adolescents. Most cats have comedones, or blackheads, on their chin. Sometimes these blackheads become infected and itchy. By scratching the spot, the cat causes a secondary inflammation and the spot becomes worse.

Mild cases are usually not even treated because they will resolve themselves, however, moderate to severe cases do require treatment. Some of the comedones (acne spots) can be so severe as to require manual expression. Shampooing with benzoyl peroxide helps flush the hair follicles; then the use of antibiotics is usually required for about three weeks. You'll need to clean kitty's chin every other day during treatment.

Q: *Our cat has suddenly lost almost all of the hair on the back two thirds of its body. Its weird. He never scratched and we don't see any sores. What could this be?*

A: There is a condition called feline endocrine alopecia that shows symptoms very much like you describe. Most veterinarians can easily recognize this when they see it, so I would encourage you to see your veterinarian as soon as you can.

The actual cause of the hair loss (alopecia) in this disease is not known, but the use of hormones will cause dramatic return of the hair! The disease is seen in both neutered males and spayed females. These cats are normal in all other respects except for the hair loss, which can be very dramatic. Typically there is no itching with this disease.

Veterinarians have attempted treatment with thyroid and testosterone hormones with only varying results. However, when the dog birth-control pill containing megestrol acetate (Ovaban) is used, hair regrows within weeks! Recently the use of this drug has become controversial among some veterinarians, so please speak with your cat's doctor and follow his advice.

Q: *We rescued a stray cat from the country yesterday. The poor thing has really bad skin problems. His whole head and ears are covered with crusty scabs, and one ear is very thick and swollen. We'll get to the vet on Monday, but is there anything we can do for him today at home?*

A: Thanks for getting this little guy some help. He probably just has a very severe case of ear mites. Ear mites live on the surface of the skin and are highly contagious to other cats. The scabs are caused by cat scratching from the intense itching caused by the mites. The thickness of one ear flap is probably a blood pocket that has formed within the ear flap itself due to severe head shaking, again caused by the intense itching.

For now you can give the little guy a good bath and gently clean out his ears with mineral oil and Q-tips. Don't probe too far down the ear canal, however, because you can cause secondary damage. Let the doctor do that. For now, get some good food in him, clean him up, use the mineral oil for cleaning the ears and any general ointment you have for the open sores.

Your veterinarian will do a good job of cleaning the ear canals and medicating the delicate tissues inside. He will probably drain the ear flap, although sometimes these blood pock-cts, called hematomas, require minor surgery for permanent correction. Follow the doctor's advice carefully on treating the mites. Mites can be persistent little devils and it is important to do the entire three-week treatment.

Q: *My cat has a funny-shaped spot on his face. The vet checked the spot with a black light and told me it was ringworm. It is not ring-shaped and it does not seem to bother the cat. Could it be something else?*

A: Sure, but it is probably ringworm. Your veterinarian has probably seen thousands of cases of ringworm, which does not always show up as a nice ring shape. If he has checked it with a Wood's lamp (or black light) then he will be pretty sure of what he is treating.

Ringworm in cats is very common and 98% of the cases are caused by one type of fungal spore. Therefore, you can feel certain your veterinarian is treating it properly.

Be sure to disinfect all your brushes and combs. All the cat's bedding should be laundered and carpets and furniture vacuumed. The vet will use some sort of topical treatment, and if the case spreads or does not improve, he may very well use oral medications as well. Some doctors like to shave the cat because so much of the fur can become contaminated with the fungus. I only shave the more severe cases.

Some ringworm cases require long-term treatment. Be prepared for many weeks of treatment, and don't get frustrated. Ask your veterinarian about a new vaccine for ringworm. It both treats active infection and prevents future cases. It's called Fel-O-Vax MC-K.

Q: *The vet says my cat has seborrhea. His skin is very oily and he feels sticky. I have some tar and sulfur shampoo from my dog who also has seborrhea? Can I use this shampoo on my cat?*

A: In dogs, seborrhea can be a primary or a secondary disease and is treated with a variety of medications, including medicated shampoos containing tar and sulfur. However, tar-based shampoos are toxic to cats, so should not be used. Shampoos containing sulfur, salicylic acid and emollients are best.

Seborrhea, as a primary disease in cats, is very rare. It is usually secondary to some other underlying disease. Therefore the underlying disease must be diagnosed and treated, then the oiliness will go away.

Be sure your veterinarian investigates other causes of this problem. The most common are: internal worms, fungal skin infections, nutritional disease, too frequent bathing, diabetes, liver disease, even feline leukemia virus infection.

PART III

BEHAVIOR AND TRAINING

CHAPTER 11

Introducing a New Pet

"Doctor Jim, we brought a new puppy into our home two weeks ago and our cat is freaked out! I don't believe his little kitty paws have set foot on solid ground since we brought the pup home. He's like Tarzan, he will go from bookshelf to chair to countertop all the way through the house. My wife wants to build him a few bridges so he can just stay up high. Now I know where the term 'catwalk' came from. Isn't there something we can do?"

How to introduce: a new baby to the cat; a new kitten to the dog; a new puppy to a cat; a new kitten to an existing cat. . . . These are frequent questions I get on talk radio.

Cats are creatures of routine and do not readily welcome change. Any addition to the family of an established, adult cat is certain to be met with some degree of resistance. It's important to consider the safety and mental well-being of both the new addition and the established pet.

Because first meetings are very important for future relationships, you must think about a plan beforehand and take your time with the introductions. Before introducing a new arrival, the whole family should sit down together for a family meeting and be instructed in THE PLAN. Then, make sure that *everybody* sticks with it.

Q: *My husband and I plan to bring home a new female kitten in a couple of weeks. We have a four-year-old, neutered male Burmese, Cocoa, who has been an "only pet." How should we introduce this new kitten?*

A: This combination should work out just fine. A kitten or a spayed adult of the opposite sex is usually best accepted by an established adult cat. Some older cats can be very intolerant of frisky kittens, but at four years old, Cocoa should enjoy playing with the newcomer, eventually. But don't expect him to be real thrilled about this interloper in the beginning. The good thing about kittens is that because they are so persistent in forcing themselves on the established cat, most younger cats, like Cocoa, will eventually succumb to their efforts to initiate play.

Try to have a friend or relative bring the new kitten into the house, so that Cocoa won't be jealous. Let the new kitten get used to your home one room at a time. Put her in a small room with her food, water, litter box, toys and bed. You can go in and visit her often, but don't force a lot of attention on her. Let her get used to you and her new surroundings at her own pace. In the meantime, Cocoa can become accustomed to her smell and sound under the door.

After the kitten has become comfortable with you and "her room" (usually two or three days), open the door and let her investigate the house. Let the kitten and Cocoa find each other with you supervising only. Do not, under any circumstances, force an introduction by picking up either or both cats and bringing them forcibly together. This is a very threatening situation for both cats. You would also be at great risk of being badly scratched.

When the cats do find each other, expect some hissing and perhaps some chasing. (Sometimes it is the adult cat who is scared of the kitten and who runs.) Try not to interfere in their encounters unless the kitten seems in danger of being injured. Do not reprimand Cocoa for any unfriendly behavior. Just try to distract him and break up any bad spats with a squirt of water. If needed, put Cocoa in a quiet room to calm down for a while.

It will probably take at least four weeks, and perhaps much longer, for Cocoa to fully accept the kitten. Be patient. Cats are slow to accept change, but Cocoa will probably be playing with the new little kitty in a couple of months.

Q: *My wife and I are soon to have our first baby. We have a two-year-old Himalayan, Fergie. Are there any special precautions to introducing her to our new baby?*

A: Congratulations on your new arrival. A new baby is an exciting event for a family, but it can mean big adjustments for a family pet. When a baby comes, there is often much less time for the family pet. You can make the transition easier for Fergie if you start preparing for it a little ahead of time. Think about how much time and attention Fergie gets now. If she is used to a lot of time with you and you know that will decrease when the baby comes, start decreasing the time you spend with her a couple of weeks before the baby comes so that she doesn't equate the arrival of the baby with the change.

VERY IMPORTANT. . . . I'm not suggesting you ignore Fergie, or relegate her to outdoors! However, if she's used to sitting in your lap for hours in the evening while you watch TV and pet her, you can start now to pet her and talk to her for several minutes, then get up and go do something. Give her lots of quality attention, but in shorter spurts.

Try *very* hard not to change the rules on her because you have a new baby. If Fergie is used to being in the house with you, don't stick her outside. She'll be very lonely and miserable. She may associate the isolation with the baby and become jealous. The most common sign of jealousy or stress in cats is elimination out of their litter box. You can avoid jealousy problems by making sure Fergie remains an important part of your family.

After the baby is born, bring an article of the baby's clothing home from the hospital and let Fergie investigate the new little one's smell ahead of time. When the baby comes home, let Fergie come up and investigate the baby while one of you holds her, if she seems to want to. Don't force an introduction by picking Fergie up and taking her up to the baby. This could be threatening to Fergie and either you or the baby could get scratched. Let Fergie investigate this newcomer at her own pace, but, of course, always supervise Fergie when she has access to the baby.

It is an old wives' tale that "cats will steal a baby's breath."

Cats do, however, sometimes like to sleep close to one's face. Small babies don't have the muscle control to be able to move their head if kitty lies up against their mouth and nose, so supervise carefully and don't let Fergie up in the crib to sleep by the baby.

Make an effort to spend some quality time playing with and petting Fergie every day. She's going to miss the attention she received before the baby came.

Most cats are wonderful with babies and accept them readily as one of the family. Once babies start crawling and toddling, though, they often become fascinated with kitty and may pull tails or poke or slap the kitty. Again, this is a time for close supervision so that Fergie isn't terrorized and baby isn't scratched out of self-defense.

Q: *How do you introduce a kitten to a dog? We have just adopted a darling mixed-breed kitten. We already have a three-year-old Boxer, Gus, who has been like our baby.*

A: Introducing a kitten to a dog usually works pretty well. It's much more difficult to get a grown cat to accept a puppy. It does help if your dog is well obedience trained, so that you can control him well, and if he has been well socialized. In other words, he was exposed to lots of people and different animals when he was a puppy and so is calm about it.

Kittens are great, because they are very persistent in approaching an older animal, but they're not big enough to be threatening to most dogs. Once properly introduced, kittens and dogs often become great friends.

When you first bring your new kitten home, let her get accustomed to her new home one room at a time. Put her in a room with her litter box, bed, food, water and toys. Let her have a day or two to settle in and get to know you before you introduce Gus. In the meantime, let Gus get used to the kitten's smell under the door.

When you first introduce Gus to the kitten, expect the kitten to do some hissing and running away. Put Gus' leash on him and have him on a down/stay if you can. Let the kitten into the room, but don't let Gus approach her. Let the kitten approach

Gus. Gus will probably whine, bark and try to rush up to the kitten. Keep him calm and make him stay with you, but don't over-reprimand him. You want his association with the kitten to be positive. Maintain a happy, positive attitude and tone of voice. Try to keep him from barking, but distract him by talking to him in an excited voice rather than reprimanding him.

The kitten will probably have hidden under a bed by now. Just stay in the room with Gus on a leash with you. Stay happy and upbeat and give the kitten time to become curious about the dog. Don't ever force the issue by holding the kitten and bringing her up to the dog or the dog up to her. This is a very threatening situation for the kitten, and you're liable to be badly scratched.

You may need to do five or six of these little sessions before the two make nose to nose contact. Let the kitten do it in her own time and supervise Gus carefully. Always praise and pet Gus when the kitten is around. This will let him know that you are happy the kitten is there and he should be too. He will also associate the praise and attention he is receiving with the cat.

Once the two have met, let the kitten have extended periods of access to the entire house while Gus stays near you on a long leash. That way, you can grab the leash and reprimand him *lightly* if he starts to chase the kitten. As long as he looks relaxed and happy, your kitten is probably not in danger. If Gus appears aggressive or nervous, then you'll need to do more sessions. Remember to praise Gus when the kitten is around and keep a happy, relaxed attitude. He takes his cues from you on how to feel about the new arrival.

Once used to each other, most dogs are good around kittens. The two often play together and may even sleep together. The kitten and Gus should be good company for each other.

Q: *We have a four-year-old mixed-breed cat, Toby, and we're bringing home a new West Highland Terrier puppy next week. How do we introduce them?*

A: This combination has a few inherent problems. Adult cats are not fond of change in their environments, and puppies are terribly rowdy. Let your cat first investigate the puppy on its own, while the puppy is in a wire puppy kennel. Most likely, the cat will want as little as possible to do with the puppy. The puppy, on the other hand, will probably be endlessly fascinated with terrorizing Toby. Let Toby avoid the puppy when he wants to. Puppies can be very rough and rowdy, and cats don't appreciate being pounced on.

You might even relax the rules a little and let Toby up on the counter in the kitchen so he can be in the kitchen with you, but be up out of puppy reach. You'll want to supervise your puppy when he is out of his kennel until he is five to six months old. Try to distract him with another activity when he takes off after the cat, but don't reprimand him. If the cat fights back and scratches him, don't interfere. Toby needs to be able to set some limits on the pup's behavior. Do check your pup carefully and see that he wasn't injured. Any actual cat scratch wounds would need immediate treatment with an antibiotic ointment.

The good news for Toby is that puppies do, eventually, grow up and become less rowdy.

Q: *My wife and I would like to adopt a young adult cat as a companion to our three-year-old silver tabby, Indy, because he is alone a lot while we're at work. How do we introduce them to each other?*

A: I think getting a feline friend for Indy is a great idea. Cats who must spend a lot of time alone can get very lonely. They also tend to become much less active and have a greater tendency to gain excess weight. Almost all cats benefit from having a feline pal.

I like the idea of your adopting a young adult cat. The shelters and humane societies are full of wonderful, healthy young adult kitties, most of whom will not find homes. These matches tend to be most successful when the new cat is the opposite sex of the existing cat and when both cats are spayed or neutered. However, almost any combination can be successful as long as both cats have been neutered or spayed. Certainly don't attempt to put two unneutered male cats together. You'll be asking for problems. If Indy isn't already neutered, have this surgery done well before you pick out your new kitty.

Before you bring your new kitty home, make sure it has been spayed or neutered, vaccinated and has tested negative for feline leukemia. Once the new kitty has a clean bill of health, have a friend or relative bring the kitty in the house, so Indy won't be jealous. Let the new kitty get used to your home one room at a time, before introducing him to Indy. Put him in a small room with his food, water, litter box, toys and bed. You can go in and visit him as much as you like, but don't force too much attention on him. Let him investigate and get comfortable with his surroundings. Don't worry if he spends the first couple of days under a bed. That is a typical "kitty reaction." He'll come out once he feels more comfortable.

In the meantime, Indy will be getting used to the smell of the new cat under the door. Don't force any investigating or interaction. Let the cats do this at their own pace.

The ideal situation is to let the new kitty take several days to become comfortable with you and with his room, and then set up a screen door over the doorway to his room so that the cats can investigate each other safely while the new cat gets to stay in his room, where he feels safe. This is certainly the safest way to introduce the cats and will prevent the established cat from attacking and chasing the newcomer, as often occurs.

Take a week to let the cats investigate each other through the screen and then open the screen door for short periods of time and let the new kitty investigate the rest of the house at his own pace. Make sure to leave the door open to his room so he can rush back in if he feels the need.

Do not, at any time, for any reason, force an introduction by picking one or both cats up and bringing them up to each other. This would be a very threatening situation for both cats and you could end up being badly scratched.

Supervise your new kitty during his early explorations out of his room. After a week of supervised explorations, you should be able to leave his room open and let him have free access to the rest of the house. Leave his food, water and litter box in his room for a while so that he has a safe, familiar place to retreat to if needed. Make sure each cat has its own food and water bowls and let them keep separate litter boxes. The smell of a strange cat in his litter box may make Indy start eliminating out of his box. Eventually, you can move the new kitty's box to another location if you wish, but let each cat keep a litter box of their own.

Don't expect the cats to take to each other right away. Do expect a certain amount of hissing and kitty karate and a lot of avoiding each other. Ignore minor skirmishes and don't reprimand either cat for any spats they might have. Do try to distract them and break up any *bad* fights by squirting the warriors with water, then wrapping them up in towels and taking them to separate rooms. Let them stay separated until they cool off. Depending on the cats, it can take from weeks to several months for cats to *fully* accept each other. Be patient. If you are careful with your introductions, they will eventually accept each other and you should notice a happier, more content and more active Indy.

CHAPTER 12

Litter Box Training and Retraining

"Doc, we've given up on our kitty using the litter box, now our shower is the box!"

"What?"

"Ally started using the bathroom in our spare shower about four months ago. We could never get her broken so we put some litter on the floor of the shower. It worked okay but now there is two inches of litter in there and we're having relatives stay with us for a week. How do I get her back in the litter box?"

By far the most common questions I get from cat owners on my national talk radio program have to do with litter box training, or the lack thereof.

I consider house soiling the most serious behavior problem in cats because it so often has fatal consequences. House soiling is the number one reason why owners give up their cats to humane societies and shelters. Most of these cats will end up being euthanized.

There are several reasons why cats start eliminating outside their litter boxes. Illnesses or changes in the cat's environment may cause the cat to start eliminating elsewhere. Whatever the initial cause, habit and the smell of previously soiled areas may lead the cat back to the inappropriate spot unless some retraining is done by the owner.

The way owners handle these occasional lapses will determine if they fix the problem or make it worse. Punishment, both verbal and especially physical punishment, has *no place* in retraining a cat to use its litter box. As a matter of fact, physical punishment has no positive purpose with cats, at all, for any reason.

Cats are complex, intelligent, sensitive creatures who are more than happy to please if their owners will do them the courtesy of explaining the rules to them in a way they can understand. Many owners actually ignore their cats most of the time when they are acting good and only interact with them to punish them when they make a mistake. It simply isn't fair to keep the rules a secret and then punish the cat for making a mistake. A lot of people think cats are aloof and uninterested in people, when in truth, the cat has learned to avoid the owner because the only time the owner interacts with the cat is to punish it.

Kittens are trained by their mother to use a litter box if left with their mother long enough and if a clean litter box is easily accessible to them. Kittens who are removed from their mothers too early, prior to eight weeks, may need some additional training to learn to use a litter box.

Q: *My husband and I have just brought home an eight-week-old Abyssinian kitten. How do we make sure, from the start, that he will use his litter box?*

A: Because your new kitten was left with his mother until he was eight weeks old, he probably has been taught by her to use a litter box. This will now need to be reinforced by you.

A new house can seem awfully big to a new little kitty and it can be hard for him to find his way back to his litter box in one part of the house. So, for the first couple of weeks, you will want to make his new environment smaller. For the first week, confine him to one small room, preferably one with a tile, wood or linoleum (nonabsorbent) floor. Put his food and water bowls, bed and toys at one end and his litter box at the other. Cats don't like to eliminate too close to where they sleep or eat, so keep some distance between the litter box and the food and bed.

Have your new kitten spend most of his time in this small enclosed area at first, where his world is small and his choices are few. Kittens begin using their litter box immediately if it is nearby and easy to get in and out of. This elimination behavior is deeply ingrained and stays with most cats all of their life.

Visit your kitten often and play with and pet him. When you see him use his litter box, praise him gently but enthusiastically and pet him. In this way, you are letting him know that you are pleased when he eliminates in his box.

Once he is well adjusted to his new room and is using his litter box very well, gradually increase the area of the house he has access to. Supervise him at first on his investigations. Make sure he always has access to "his room." If it is in a bathroom, make sure the door can't accidentally get shut and leave him unable to get to his box.

As he is allowed to romp through the entire house, the natural instinct to eliminate in one spot will draw him back to "his spot" and he will trot back to his litter box when his little bladder is full. If your house is large, it's a good idea to have two litter boxes, one at each end of the house, especially while he is little.

Q: *A month ago I got a new kitten. She was only five weeks old when I brought her home from the pet shop. She uses her litter box consistently, but the problem is . . . well, she doesn't cover her "stuff" up. Why do you think that is? Is there anyway to teach her to cover it?*

A: Actually, what you describe is a common problem in kittens who are taken away from their mothers too early. Five weeks is way too young. Ideally, a kitten should stay with its mother until it is eight weeks old.

Your kitten is using her litter box because nature tells her to pick an absorbent surface and to return to the same place each time she eliminates. However, she wasn't with her mother long enough to learn the finer points of "feline litter box etiquette."

This can be a difficult, if not impossible situation to "cure." You'll need to make an effort to be present as often as possible when your kitten eliminates. The best way to do this is to feed her on a regular schedule and notice when she typically defecates. When you notice your kitten using her litter box, wait until she has finished and then, while she is still in the box, gently and quietly encourage her to scratch the litter by taking the litter scoop and carefully flicking litter over the feces. You can also gently take her front foot and move it in a scratching motion on the litter. If she makes *any* attempt to scratch, gently but enthusiastically praise her, pet her and give her a little treat, such as cheese or liver.

You will need to be very gentle with all of this so as not to scare her and make her afraid of her litter box. If she runs out of the box, you've been too aggressive. The last thing you want is to make her avoid her box altogether.

Probably the most practical solution is to adjust yourself to the situation and simply pick out the feces when you notice (or smell) them in the box. Keep a supply of little plastic bags near the box and scoop the feces out, bag them and throw them away. Litter boxes should be picked out daily. A dirty litter box is very offensive to a cat and can cause it to start eliminating outside its box.

Q: *My six-year-old Russian Blue, Sapphire, has always used her litter box just fine. All of the sudden, she has started to urinate on my bath mat. I've scolded and spanked her and washed the bath mat every time I found urine on it, but the problem just seems to be getting worse. What can I do?*

A: When a cat has been using its litter box well for six years and then suddenly starts eliminating out of its box, I would suspect that an illness or a change in its environment has upset it. Is there a new pet or new person in the house?

Why yes, I just got a new Golden Retriever puppy a month ago. Up until then, Sapphire had been an "only pet."

Cats are creatures of habit and can become quite undone over major environment changes, like the sudden arrival of a large, boisterous puppy. One way cats react to stressful changes is to start eliminating out of their litter boxes. The way you react to this problem will either fix the problem or make it worse. Unfortunately, you have done exactly the wrong thing.

First of all, cats do not respond at all well to punishment, especially *physical* punishment like spanking. She also is unable to associate the punishment with the accident, which may have occurred several minutes or even hours before you found it. All you have done is to increase her stress. In her mind, not only have you brought an extremely boisterous wolf into her peaceful home, but you have also gone crazy and occasionally yell at her and hit her for no reason. Not to mention that she is probably not getting anywhere near the amount of attention she is used to getting from you now that your energy is consumed with raising a puppy. So, you can see that, from her perspective, life has fallen apart.

Now, the good news is that most adult cat house soiling problems are short-term and will clear up just fine if you handle the problem properly. Cats are extremely fastidious and will usually revert back to their normal, clean elimination habits once they have adjusted to the change in their environment. To handle this type of house soiling problem, you need to follow these rules.

- The first rule is: NO PUNISHMENT. You don't want to make matters worse, and that is exactly what punishment does.
- The second rule is: Regular sessions of attention and play. Set aside a couple of times a day when you focus all your attention on Sapphire and hold her, pet her and play with her. As she adjusts to the new puppy, she may not require as much attention, but she certainly needs reassurance from you right now.
- The third rule is confinement retraining: Confine Sapphire to a small room with her food, water, toys and bed at one end and her litter box at the other. It helps if the floor is nonabsorbent, such as tile, wood or linoleum. Cats like to eliminate on absorbent surfaces, so try to make her litter box the only absorbent surface in the room, other than her bed. Cats don't like to eliminate close to where they sleep or eat, so put the litter box at the opposite end of the room from the food, water, toys and bed.

  Keep the litter box well cleaned. Cats are naturally very clean, and a dirty litter box may make them start eliminating out of the box. I like to use clumping-type cat litters so that the urine as well as the feces can be picked out daily.

  Visit Sapphire often, and let her have short excursions out of her room when you can supervise her. When you can't watch her, she needs to be in her room. Within one to two weeks, most cats will have focused their elimination habits back to their litter box and can be allowed gradual access to the whole house again.

- The fourth rule is: Completely remove the odor from any accident spots. While she is in "kitty confinement camp," you will need to carefully clean any areas where she may have urinated with an enzyme odor remover. Don't use ammonia or other cleaning agents as their strong smell may only attract her to the area. Use an enzyme odor remover, such as Nature's Miracle or Outright, to completely remove any trace of the smell. These are available at pet stores and some discount stores. Be sure to use these on any puppy accident spots as well. The odor of puppy urine or feces may cause Sapphire to use those spots.

- And finally, rule five: Make sure Sapphire has a place to go to get away from the puppy when she wants to. Her litter box certainly needs to be where the puppy can't get to her while she's trying to use it. You may want to put her litter box in a laundry room or bathroom and install a cat door on the door to the room so that you can leave the door closed to prevent the puppy from entering, but Sapphire can have free access.

   You may also want to relax the rules a bit to allow Sapphire access to the kitchen counter so that she can be where you are, but stay out of puppy reach.

Q: *My wife and I have a two-year-old tabby. He is a neutered male and has always used his litter box reliably. We went on a three-week vacation a couple of weeks ago and left him at home with a neighbor coming in to feed him every day. Since we got back, he hasn't been using his litter box. Why do you suppose he would suddenly stop using his box?*

A: There are a variety of reasons why a cat will suddenly stop using his litter box. These reasons can be broken down into four categories.

   1. His litter box has become unappealing for some reason. The most common reason a litter box becomes unappealing is

because it becomes too dirty. Cats are very fastidious creatures and will often stop using a box if it becomes too dirty or smells too bad.

Other things that can make a cat's litter box unappealing to him are changes in the type of litter, a new cat using his box, a change of box location, too much activity near the box and not enough privacy and quiet.

Some owners actually take advantage of their cats in the litter box by choosing that time to grab them to give medications or apply flea spray. Cats will quickly pick another spot to eliminate if they can't have some peace and privacy in their litter box.

2. Another spot has become more appealing. Unless you have taken the time to praise your cat for going in his box, he is most likely unaware that you prefer he eliminate there. He may become interested in the dirt in the pot of a large plant, or the scent of a prior accident may cause him to return to a previously soiled spot or he could just prefer the texture of another spot.

3. He is experiencing stress caused by change in environment or routine. While we don't know exactly why stress causes a cat to start eliminating out of his litter box, we do know without a doubt that stress is one of the big causes. This is yet another reason why punishing a cat for house soiling is not only ineffective, but makes the problem worse. Cats do not respond well to punishment, especially physical punishment. As a matter of fact, physical punishment for other misbehaviors often causes a cat to start eliminating out of its box.

Any major change in a cat's environment, such as the addition of a new pet or a new spouse may set off house soiling. A major change in the cat's routine, especially if it is prolonged, may also cause enough stress to trigger house soiling.

4. He is ill. Some illness, such as bladder infections, feline urological syndrome (FUS) or diarrhea, may cause a cat to be unable to control its bowels or bladder. Once an "accident" has occurred, the cat may return to use the spot because he can smell his scent there. Habit may also cause the cat to return to a previously soiled spot.

It could be that your neighbor didn't keep your cat's box clean while you were gone, or perhaps she brought her dog over to the house with her. Your cat could have been stressed over your long absence, or he could have a bladder infection or FUS.

Whatever the reason, you should be able to fix the problem by correcting any obvious reasons he may have rejected his box (remember that it may be a medical cause that will require your veterinarian's expertise), then retraining him to his litter box using the confinement method, and finally treating all soiled spots in the house with a good enzyme odor remover.

Q: I've listened to your show many times, and I've heard you talk about "confinement retraining" to teach a cat to start using its litter box again. How exactly is that done?

A: Occasionally a cat, for one reason or another, decides another spot is preferable to its litter box. Then, because of the habitual nature of elimination, that spot is used repetitively. Unfortunately that spot may be your bed, favorite chair or dining room carpet.

To get your cat to use his box again, you must refocus his elimination behavior back to the approved spot, his litter box. I call it "confinement retraining," or refocusing.

Here's how:

Just pretend your adult cat is a kitten again. Put him in a small room with food, water, toys, sleeping materials at one end and a litter box at the other. This helps take advantage of the cat's normal tendency to eliminate away from where he eats.

The room should have a tile, wood or linoleum floor so that the only thing in the environment that is absorbent is the litter box. In a matter of a few hours to days, 98% of all cats are going back in the box. I suggest you allow this to become affixed in his little kitty mind for several days, up to two weeks, then slowly allow him the right to enter the rest of the house.

Now, while he is away at kitty camp, you are busy, too. During the time your cat is in the confinement area, you need to get on your hands and knees and find each and every spot he has used. Then treat the spot with an enzyme odor remover.

These odor removers are the only thing that will completely remove all the waste odors and therefore not allow the cat to find the unapproved spot.

After you have treated the spot well, I also suggest you simply block off the area with a plant or chair so the location is not only odor free, but is physically inaccessible. This combined with the confinement retraining will cure 99% of cats who have house soiled.

Please remember that if the problem is persistent, it may be a medical problem, as cats are quite prone to bladder infections and, of course, FUS. So a trip to the veterinarian may very well be in order. However, most of these cases are behavioral and not medical. Therefore they require behavioral treatments and not medical treatments.

Finally, try to figure out why your cat may have stopped using his box and try to correct the problem.

Q: *My four-year-old Siamese has started not using her litter box. She has had occasional accidents in the past, once when she was sick and a couple of times when she accidentally got closed up away from her box. This is the first time she has stopped using her box altogether. I know I need to "confinement retrain" her, I've heard you talk about that a lot. How can I prevent this from happening again?*

A: Cats are such creatures of habit and routine, they hate it when things change. Therefore, if the box has changed locations, or the litter has changed types, or you have changed schedules—any of these things can cause your cat to stop using her litter box. *So*, you need to try to determine what has changed and, if possible, get it back to the way it was.

Of course many times this is impossible, like when you move to a new home or apartment. If so, the confinement retraining method will most times refocus a cat's elimination behavior back to its litter box.

Be sure to carefully clean all spots where your kitty has had accidents. Use a good enzyme odor remover to completely remove the smell so that your cat is not attracted back to the spot.

To avoid future problems, make sure your cat's box is always clean. Cats do not like to eliminate in a dirty litter box. Other things that cause cats to go outside the box are competition from other cats, new pets in the house and not enough quiet and privacy at the litter box location.

If you change litter, do it slowly, mixing small amounts of new litter in with the old until you have gradually switched to the new litter. If you change litter suddenly, the smell and feel of the new litter may cause your cat to reject the box in favor of a corner behind the couch.

Cats' paws are incredibly sensitive. Some cats don't like the way a litter feels, especially those who have access to outdoors. They may be going in a sandy area or a flower bed during the day and may find the litter in their box funny-feeling and may decide not to use it for that reason. Before the advent of the new clumping cat litters, I corrected this problem by simply putting sand or dirt in the litter box. The cats would immediately begin using the box again.

Clumping litters feel so much like sand that most cats will use them right away. Also, clumping cat litters are very convenient. If you have not tried them yet, do so! You probably will never go back to regular cat litter again. When urine hits this type of litter, it balls up into a clump which can be easily lifted out. Nothing is left behind but clean litter, which is pretty much odor free. Both feces and urine balls should be scooped out daily, and new litter should be added when needed.

CHAPTER 13

Behavior Problems and Aggression

*"Dr. Jim, my wife's cat has a real behavior problem and I
need to cure it."*

   "What's the problem?"

   *"It plays all the time—it just won't stop! I need some
sleep. This cat bounces all over the bed at 3 AM, and I just
can't take it anymore. Help!"*

Behavior problems constitute a large percentage of the calls I get
on talk radio. This is not surprising when you realize that almost
all pet owners report some sort of undesirable behavior in their
pets. As a matter of fact, behavior problems are the number one
reason why pets, both dogs and cats, are given up to shelters and
humane societies. Tragically, most of these pets will be euthanized. It is shocking, sad and unnecessary. Most all behavior
problems are preventable or correctable. It only takes some effort
and commitment on the part of the pet owner.

The good news for cat owners is that cats tend to have many
fewer behavior problems than dogs, as well as less destructive
and dangerous behavior problems.

Cats also respond very differently to training methods than
dogs do. Dogs, being pack animals by nature, look to a "pack
leader" for instruction and approval. Cats are not pack animals
by nature and do not form dominance–submission hierarchies.
They do not respond to the same sort of training methods that are
most effective in dogs. Therefore, we must use different techniques for training cats and for correcting behavior problems.

One thing is the same, ncither dogs or cats respond well to physical punishment. Cats, especially, do not respond well to any type of hitting or spanking. Physical punishment will make an aggressive cat more aggressive and a timid, scared cat more timid and scared.

I receive a fair number of calls regarding aggression in cats. Aggression problems in cats are very different from aggression problems in dogs. Dogs interact with other dogs and with humans as part of a "pack." Disagreements occur and are settled according to positions of dominance and submission. Cats do not see themselves as pack members, certainly not submissive pack members. Cats consider themselves equal to (or superior to) all other life forms, including humans. It's part of why we love them.

Because they are so different from dogs, aggression problems in cats must also be handled quite differently than aggression problems in dogs. Many aggression problems in cats are caused by rough handling. Cats do not respond favorably to physical punishment or to rough play. Cats do respond very well to patient, kind and fair treatment.

Q: *My wife and I have a two-year-old Burmese, Sheba. We love her dearly, but she does have one bad habit. She sharpens her claws on our couch. She's really made a mess out of one corner. How can we break her of this?*

A: Scratching on the furniture is the second most common complaint among cat owners. As common as this complaint is, I have found it one of the most simple behavior problems to correct.

Remember that in the wild, cats mark their territory both with urine and with the scent that is secreted from their foot pads when they scratch an object. While not detected by you, this scent serves as a signpost to other cats of a territorial boundary.

Cats are also very smart animals who like to please. By simple negative and positive reinforcement, most cats can be trained to do all their scratching on a scratching post and nowhere else.

Here's how you do it. Obviously the best time to start is

when your cat is a young kitten, but you can use the same technique on adult cats. When your cat starts to scratch in an unapproved area, use loud clapping or a loud, sharp *no* to startle it and interrupt its scratching. A spray of water from a plant mister works well to stop scratching. Just be sure to stop spraying as soon as the cat stops scratching. The idea is to startle the cat into stopping scratching, that's all.

Don't yell at the cat, and try not to scare it, or you won't be able to accomplish the next step, which is to calmly and gently guide your cat over to its scratching post and place its feet on the post. You can encourage your cat to scratch by acting out scratching by running your fingers up and down the post. While you may feel a little silly doing this, it works great. The other essential thing to do is to praise your kitty and pet it while it is at its scratching post.

Make the scratching post very attractive and convenient to your cat. Tying a catnip mouse on the post does wonders in terms of attracting the cat to the post. You can also rub catnip on the post, or use catnip spray, available from your pet shop. Praise your kitty every time you see it scratching or playing on its scratching post.

Meanwhile, back at the scene of the crime, I suggest you treat the area of your couch that your cat tends to scratch with an enzyme odor remover to remove the territorial scent. Then make the surface unappealing for scratching by covering the area with aluminum foil or plexiglass. You can also spray the area with a pet repellent, available from your pet store. You'll need to respray everyday for several weeks until the habit is broken.

Q: *Is one scratching post enough for a multi-cat house? I have three kitties. Also, where's the best place to put the scratching post?*

A: Where you put the post is important. It should be convenient for your cats, so choose a location where your cats spend a lot of time. Cats like to scratch after waking from a nap, so it's a good idea to have a post near where your cats like to sleep. In a large home or in homes with more than one cat, it's a good idea to have several scratching posts or cat furniture in different areas of the home. Cat furniture, with shelves for the cat to get on, is a great idea because cats will sleep on them, then when waking will stretch and scratch. Soon it becomes habit for the cats to scratch on their own cat furniture.

Q: I love my two cats, but I wish I could teach them to stay off my kitchen counters. Do you have any suggestions?

A: Cats live by certain rules. One of those rules is to get on the highest object in their immediate area and act superior.

In keeping with this cat rule, kitchen counter tops are prime real estate for house cats. This creates a problem since most of us don't want cat hair in our cookies, not to mention the dangers that are present on kitchen counters, like knives and hot stove tops.

When you're at home and catch one of your cats on the counter, use a squirt of water from a plant mister to startle him and send him off the counter. Say a loud, sharp, *"No, get down,"* just before you squirt him. Soon, he'll fly off the counter with the verbal reprimand alone. With consistency, he'll stop getting up on the counter (when you're around).

This works well while you're home, but when you are off to work, the cats may be dancing happily on the counter tops. I've found that cookie sheets filled with water placed over most of the counter surface will break this habit. Other things that work are pet repellent sprays, sprayed on bath towels then placed on the counters, or sheets of aluminum foil laid on the counters. One very effective retraining device for cats getting on unapproved surfaces is the Scat Mat, made by Contec Electronics. It delivers a harmless tingle when your cat lands on it. It can be placed on furniture, counter tops, car hoods, anywhere you want to break the kitty traffic pattern. You can find the Scat Mat at some pet stores, but it is available nationwide by mail order by calling (800) 767-8658.

With all these methods, consistency is the key. Be prepared to use these methods of training for at least four to six weeks.

Q: My four-month-old mixed-breed kitten is chewing little holes in the blanket on my daughter's bed. She doesn't chew on anything

else, but I can't get her to leave the blanket alone. What can I do
to break her of this?

A: Chewing is not usually a big problem in cats (except with houseplants). It does occasionally occur, however. This problem typically occurs in kittens and tends to be focused on one particular object or type of material. Your kitten probably finds the texture and feel of your daughter's blanket particularly inviting.

There are two ways to approach curing the problem. The simplest is to restrict the kitten's access to the blanket. Close the door of your daughter's room so the kitten can't get to the blanket, or cover the blanket with a comforter or spread.

If restricting the kitten's access to the blanket is not practical for some reason, then treat the chewed areas with some bad-tasting stuff like Bitter Apple or Chew Stop. You can buy these sprays at your pet store. Spray the chewed areas each day for at least two to three weeks to break the habit.

Q: *I have tried everything to teach my cat to use a scratching post, but he still insists on scratching on the door frames or windowsills. Do you have any suggestions?*

A: Sometimes the key is finding the right scratching surface for your cat. Not all cats prefer to scratch on carpet. Some prefer other surfaces such as wood or upholstery. There are many different types of scratching pads and scratching posts you can purchase or make from sisal rope, burlap, carpet or pressure-treated wood left natural. Almost all cats seem to love the corrugated cardboard scratch pads filled with catnip. These cardboard scratch pads are fairly inexpensive compared to scratching posts, but you'll need to replace them more often.

Try providing your cat with a variety of approved scratching surfaces. Once you find one he likes, keep a couple in different areas of the house. Pick places your cat likes to spend time in, especially where he likes to sleep.

Q: *My tortoiseshell kitty, Lila, comes to life late at night. Just about the time I get to sleep, she starts playing all over the bed. She even carries toys up into bed and drops them on my face, trying to get me to play with her. I don't want to have to shut her out of the room at night, is there a way to break her of this?*

A: Cats are nocturnal animals. They love to hunt and play at night. If they are not really hunting, then they are practicing, just in case.

This is not to say that these little furry nocturnal creatures can't learn to adapt to our schedule. What happens in most cases is that the cat is left alone all day while her owners are at work. The kitty tends to sleep all day long and is ready to get up and play at night.

I suggest you be sure to give your kitty some good attention when you get home from work. Then, shortly before you go to bed, get your kitty to play vigorously until she is tired. Literally wear her out just before bedtime each night. Make a home-made cat toy of a piece of cloth, or use a catnip toy on a string. Most cats can't resist the movement. You should be able to wear her out without a problem. She should then let you sleep at night. She'll also start to really look forward to your play sessions. Cats love having special routines with their owners. With some effort on your part, you should be able to get her schedule to coincide with yours.

Q: *I have a new kitten. He is adorable and very loving, but I have never seen such an energetic and active animal. He is in constant motion. How do I teach him to not tear up my furniture, drapes, plants, etc.?*

A: One of the special joys of having a kitten is watching it play, but some kittens are perpetual motion machines with no "off switch." Kittens are like human toddlers, full of excess energy, intense curiosity and no ability to fully understand yet what is appropriate behavior and what is not. Be patient. The good news is that he will calm down as he matures.

Try to prevent problems rather than punishing mistakes. For a while, put up breakables, take plants into a room you can close off from the kitten and spread a plastic drop cloth over furniture he seems to want to scratch on. Keep his nails trimmed every week. This will keep the sharp edges off and lessen damage to you, your clothing and your furniture. Make sure he has plenty of cat toys to play with and a couple of fun scratching posts he can climb and play on.

You may want to seriously consider getting another kitten as a companion for this little guy. A kitten with this much energy could really benefit from a playmate to chase, wrestle and play with. Growing up together, they will be very bonded and will be good company for each other their whole lives.

Q: *My husband and I have just adopted a new kitten. The problem is our other cat, Spider. Spider is five years old, and we've had him since kittenhood. He wants nothing to do with this new kitten. He attacks it whenever he sees it. What's going on with him?*

A: Spider is exhibiting territorial aggression. Cats, as a group, are very uncomfortable with change. Since Spider hasn't been exposed to other cats since he was a kitten, he has become very used to being the only cat in his territory. The new kitten is seen as an intruder, and Spider is trying to chase him off. You will want to closely supervise their interactions for several weeks until Spider gets used to the idea of this newcomer. While the kitten is small, Spider could injure him.

Don't punish Spider for aggression, but supervise things so that you can rescue the kitten if necessary. It's important to start this new relationship off on the right foot, so read Chapter 11 for more details on how to introduce a new kitten to an established cat.

Q: *I have a ten-year-old Turkish Angora. She is very affectionate to me, although she prefers to avoid strangers. My sister and eighteen-month-old niece were visiting yesterday when Sassy dashed out from under the couch, bit my niece on the leg, and ran back under the couch. It was a bad bite, leaving four tooth holes. I've never seen her attack anyone like that before. What do you think caused it?*

A: While some cats are completely unperturbed by visitors and new situations, some cats are totally undone by strangers in their environment. Sassy was exhibiting territorial aggression and was trying to chase off the intruder. Not being used to small children, she may have considered your niece another animal because it is very unusual for cats to exhibit territorial aggression toward people. Most cats afraid of strangers will simply run and hide until the strangers are gone. Because toddlers walk very differently from adults and older children and make very different sounds, they are not always recognized by animals to be human. It's therefore very important to supervise these young kids around pets.

Now that you know that Sassy perceives your niece as an intruder to her territory, it would be a good idea to close Sassy in the safety of your bedroom or some other favorite place when your niece comes to visit, at least until your niece gets older.

Q: *Our one-year-old female cat is spayed. She likes to go outside, but lately she has been getting into fights with a cat that comes into our backyard. We're having to treat her now for bite-wound abscesses. I didn't think spayed females fought. What's going on?*

A: Although the most common and severe fighting between cats occurs between intact males, any cat may fight to chase intruders out of its territory. Cats tend to be possessive of their own turf. This is a matter to be concerned about. Cats that go outside and are exposed to other cats are at much greater risk for contracting diseases such as leukemia. Injuries from fights can also be quite severe. While I understand why you like to let your cat go outside, she will be much safer and most likely live longer if you keep her inside. For more on the benefits of keeping cats indoors, see Chapter 23.

Q: *I have an eighteen-month-old male cat named Magic. Magic has been getting in some serious cat fights the last couple of months. I've had him to the vet five times and he's starting to cost me a fortune. He also disappears for days at a time. How can I break him of this?*

Is he neutered?

No.

A: Here are the facts of cat life. Unneutered male cats typically live very short, very dangerous lives. As an intact male, Magic is exhibiting intermale aggression. An intact male will roam looking for females, and he will fight, very seriously, with other intact males he encounters. He can't help this, he is a slave to his hormones. Neutering stops 90% of all intermale aggression either immediately or within a few weeks of surgery.

The cure for your problems is this:
1. Have Magic neutered immediately.
2. Make him an indoor cat. He will be safe and will be a much better, more affectionate pet (not to mention less expensive). Intact male cats spend most of their time distracted over females. Neutered males are happier, more relaxed and more interactive with people.

Q: *My four-year-old tabby gets very aggressive when I take him to the veterinarian. He yowls, bites and scratches at the vet and the technician. He never did this until two years ago when he went through extensive treatment for a blocked urinary tract. He is still sweet and loving at home. Why does he get so out of sorts at the veterinary clinic?*

A: This is an example of fear-induced aggression. This occurs when a cat is afraid of a situation and would escape if he could. If he cannot escape, he turns to aggression to try to drive the tormentor away long enough for him to escape. Cats are, by nature, not naturally aggressive to people. If afraid, most will simply run and hide. If prevented from escaping, however, cats can get pretty aggressive. They will be only as aggressive as needed in order to get a chance to escape, and seldom will pursue and fight.

It is very common for cats to exhibit fear-induced aggression following some sort of bad experience. For example, a cat who has been badly treated by a man may be fearful of men, but not women.

In the case of your cat, he associates going to the veterinarian with the unpleasantness of his treatment two years ago. Because he is forced into this fearful situation and is unable to escape, he becomes aggressive. Your veterinarian may want to tranquilize your cat if he has much work to do on him. Tranquilizing may decrease his fear reaction and help him get used to going to the vet.

In cats who are severely aggressive going to the veterinarian, it sometimes helps to have a house-call veterinarian see your cat in his own house. There are a growing number of "mobile veterinarians." You might see if there is one in your area.

Q: *I have a ten-year-old Calico Angora. When she was a kitten, my brother teased her a lot. Since then she has been very afraid of men. She is very affectionate and loving to me but doesn't like strangers. I recently got married and my husband can't even touch Sheba without her attacking him. Her bites are very serious. What can we do?*

A: Sheba has a severe fear-induced aggression. In most fear-induced problems in cats it's best to just avoid the fearful thing. However, since Sheba and your new husband are going to be living together, you'll need to get her over her fear of him.

This is going to be hard on you, but I promise it really works. My wife had a severely aggressive cat when we got married, and it worked on her.

You should stop all affection and feeding of Sheba. (Don't panic, it's just until she gets over this.) Your husband will take over all feeding, and any attention must come from him. Sheba is not going to be the least bit interested in attention from your husband if she is still getting attention from you, so YOU MUST TOTALLY IGNORE HER. Don't look at her. Don't talk to her. Don't pet her or let her get on your lap. Don't let her sleep by you, *nothing!*

In addition to feeding her, your husband can offer her tasty little treats of cheese or meat a couple of times a day. If she appears calm, he should try to pet her, but if she shows any aggressive behavior (growling, hissing, ears back, biting or scratching), he should stand up, turn around and walk away. Do not physically punish her for aggressive behavior, as that will make the problem much worse. Just stand up, turn around and walk away. The message to Sheba is this: you get attention on my terms, or not at all.

If she is not getting any attention from you, she will eventually seek out your husband. If he stops all attention when she gets aggressive, she will learn that she has to be nice or he ignores her.

Be prepared to follow this plan for several weeks, maybe even a month. It works well, but it takes time. Good luck!

Q: *My husband and I have a two-year-old Siamese, Dahlila. She is very nervous when our grandchildren are around, but she won't go off by herself. She has to be in the middle of everything we're doing. Last weekend she bit our four-year-old granddaughter, who was pulling on her tail. What should we do to prevent this happening again?*

A: This is an example of pain-induced aggression. Cats don't typically initiate aggression against humans. Children, however, may be too rough with a cat, pulling its hair or tail, or playing too roughly with it. Cats will respond to pain by lashing out suddenly and biting or scratching. Most cats will scratch first, but declawed cats will learn to bite for self-defense.

Teach your grandchildren how to pet the cat gently and to *never* pull on it or poke at it. Supervise the interactions between the grandkids and the cat from now on, and make sure Dahlila has a place she can get away to that is off limits to the kids.

Q: *A couple of weeks ago my cat was hit by a car. When I went to pick her up she bit me very badly. She has never been a bit aggressive. Did I do something to cause her to bite?*

A: This is a very common example of pain-induced aggression. Cats react to fear and pain by scratching or biting in response. An injured cat, or any pet, will bite even its owner out of fear and pain. This is a good thing to keep in mind if your pet is injured. Try to move her in such a way as to avoid being bitten or scratched. A large towel placed over an injured cat can help, and thick gloves are another good idea.

Q: *Our two-year-old, neutered male tabby is a real hunter. He's not real popular with the neighbors, though, because he kills so many birds. I don't know how to stop him from hunting. Can you help?*

A: Predatory aggression is part of being a cat for most cats, although there are some domesticated cats who wouldn't know what to do with a mouse. Predatory aggression isn't all bad in cats either. A cat's ability to keep down mouse and rat populations is well appreciated in many settings.

For suburban house cats, though, hunting can make them unpopular. The easiest and best way to stop hunting is to keep your cat indoors. Indoor cats do live longer, healthier lives. If that is not an option, you can put a bell on his collar. That may warn some of the adult birds before he can sneak up on them. You can ask your neighbors to spray him with a water hose if they see him hunting in their yard. If he is terrorizing a particular nest, try sabotaging the area around the base of the tree with mouse traps set and turned upside down. He'll set them off if he goes through the area, but he won't be hurt.

Q: *Our family has a four-year-old Maine Coon and a Cockatiel. The Cockatiel is kept in a cage on a dresser in my daughter's bedroom. Anytime her door is left open, Max tears in there and attacks the cage. How can I get him to leave the poor bird alone?*

A: It's not really possible to stop predatory aggression in a cat that loves to hunt, but there are a couple of things you can do to maintain peace in the family. First, make sure that the bird is caged as safely as possible. Consider hanging his cage from the ceiling, far enough away from furniture that Max can't leap for the cage and get it. Make sure the cage door closes securely and can't come open if the cage gets knocked over.

Keep a spray bottle, filled with water, handy near the bird cage. If Max goes for the cage, spray him with the water. Cats hate to get sprayed with water and will usually take off for other parts of the house. Be prepared to repeat this exercise many times before he starts to avoid the cage.

If you can't hang the cage, sabotage the area around it with mouse traps set and turned upside down. He'll set off the traps and startle himself if he gets around the cage. There are also some commercially available products that work well. I like the Scat Mat. It is a mat that delivers a very small, harmless shock when the cat jumps up on it. You could place it in front of the cage and it would definitely keep Max off the dresser. You would need to leave it in place several weeks to make sure Max continues to avoid the area.

Q: *My male cat is very affectionate and loves to be petted, but sometimes he will rub up against me and ask to be petted, let me pet him for a minute and then bite me or scratch me. How can I stop this?*

A: This affection-related aggression is not uncommon. It seems to happen most often in male cats, either neutered or intact. They obviously want to be petted, seem to enjoy the attention, but then suddenly become uncomfortable with it and bite or scratch.

This aggression seems especially common when the cat is petted on his stomach even though he has turned over on his back and asked for it. I'd suggest you limit your petting to your cat's head and back and don't pet him on the stomach. Learn to read his body language and try to anticipate when he's had enough attention. Watch for his ears to go back, and for his eyes to focus on your hand. When you see these things, stop the petting, stand up and walk away.

If you don't stop in time and he does bite you, don't physically punish him. That does no good. Just stand up, walk away and ignore him. That's the best way to deal with aggression in cats.

PART IV

FLEAS, TICKS AND WORMS

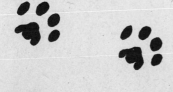

CHAPTER 14

"Miracle" Cures and the Four Steps of *Real* Flea Control

"Dr. Jim, I've always heard that garlic cures worms in cats, but how do you get a cat to eat garlic?"

I am no longer surprised at the number of old wives' tales about simple foods, herbs and household products having incredible effects on certain medical conditions. While I do believe some of these home remedies have some effect, often minimal, I feel that too many people rely on these things as cures. I do not discourage the use of home remedies as long as they do no harm. Some, however, are very harmful or at best, are simply an exercise in futility.

Q: I've heard that garlic will cure flea problems and kill worms. Is that true?

A: Garlic powder does seem to stimulate finicky eaters to eat better, but I do not believe that garlic, by itself, will cure fleas or worms or any other ailment. I usually don't discourage use of garlic as long as some conventional medications are used along with the garlic. Of course, I know that if the medication has its purported effect, the cat owner will give the credit to the garlic.

Q: How about brewer's yeast? Does it help in flea control?

A: Brewer's yeast is another ingredient often touted as being "the flea cure." There are even several manufacturers that produce

131

commercially available mixtures of brewer's yeast and other compounds you can buy for your cat. Brewer's yeast is full of B-complex vitamins and is certainly a good supplemental source of vitamin B for cats, but it should not be touted as a cure for fleas or anything else.

Q: *We do not want to use harsh chemicals around our house, certainly not on our Persian cats. We currently give them brewer's yeast and garlic tablets, plus eucalyptus oil put on a bandanna tied around their necks. What we can do to kill fleas in the carpet?*

A: If you have only a mild flea problem, you can probably continue to get good control using these kinds of nontraditional, nonchemical modes of flea repellers. If, however, you develop a moderate to severe flea problem, all the garlic and eucalyptus you could find probably won't help.

You will need the help of modern chemicals like insect growth regulators and you will need to undertake the four-step flea control program (outlined in this chapter) and get an initial knock-down of the flea population. Then, once the fleas are somewhat under control, you can continue the nonchemical methods of repelling fleas.

The nonchemical, nontoxic methods I like and that are proven to be effective are the use of diatomaceous earth in the yard and sodium borate dusted into the carpet. Be sure you use diatomaceous earth made for organic gardening and not for swimming pools. The sodium borate will help prevent larval development in your carpet for up to one full year.

Q: *My mother bought an electronic flea collar from a catalogue. Do those things really work?*

A: Every ultrasonic device I've seen and tested for flea control does not work. I've written and called many of the manufacturers for test results, and so far I have received only testimonials from "satisfied customers." While testimonials are fine, they are not proof.

I've tried ultrasonic devices on my pets and have had friends and clients test them. I've even sent samples in to universities for testing. So far, no one reports success.

I can tell you that after six years of talk radio, I have spoken with no one who has called my show to say how well these products work. I have spoken with about five manufacturers about their products. They have five different explanations of how their products work. So far no one has provided independent scientific data as proof. It's a totally unproved gimmick.

I would like to believe it works. I would like us to have a nonchemical method of true flea control. However, mild levels of ultrasonic waves, produced by a small ceramic speaker aimed at right angles to the cat's neck just do not work.

Q: *Our vet has told us there is a new cure for fleas in cats. He said it was just a single drop of a special chemical put on the cat's forehead. Have you ever heard of that?*

A: Oh yes, and I recommend you avoid this treatment in favor of more traditional modes of flea control. This is a very concentrated, highly toxic organophosphate chemical called fenthion. It was initially formulated so that only very small amounts could be poured on to the backs of cattle to rid them of parasites. It is not made for cats, licensed for cats, tested on cats or concentrated for cats and, therefore, should not be used on cats. In fact, some breeds of cats that are particularly sensitive to organophophates, such as Persians, may even have a fatal reaction to fenthion!

Q: *My parents used to feed our cats a mixture of garlic, plants and ash from burnt wood to treat for worms. Do you think that works?*

A: Just about the time I think I've heard it all, someone will call with another treatment for worms. I should really keep track of all of these and investigate where they come from.

No! I don't think it would work and I would be afraid of what the mixture would do to your cat's stomach, intestines, kidneys and liver. I'm not even sure what is in this concoction, but I am sure I don't want you feeding it to your cat.

Why not visit your friendly veterinary clinic and ask for a deworming pill? If you know your doctor well and he knows your pets, he may prescribe something simple without seeing the cat if the symptoms you describe are obvious (like visible tape worm segments).

If the doctor is not well familiar with you and your pet, or the symptoms are unclear, he will probably need to see your cat first. Veterinarians do not give any kind of medication for conditions that are not well diagnosed.

Q: *My mother went to a big pet show and came home with some stuff in a bottle for fleas. We are supposed to just wipe it on the cat's fur and the fleas die. What is that?*

A: I do not know, but I am always leery of anything you put on cats. As you know, cats spend most of their day grooming themselves. Therefore, anything you put on a cat will end up in its system. Anything in a bottle that is strong enough to kill fleas by simply being wiped on is probably toxic to the cat and should be used with caution.

Also, the problem with these cures is that they ignore the four-step process of flea control. Even if you did get rid of the fleas on the cat, they are still in the carpet, and in the grass and will reinfest the kitty in a matter of hours. Please don't be lead astray by "miracle cures" that sound too good to be true. They are.

Q: *We were in the pet store yesterday buying food and yet another cat toy, and my wife mentioned that our cat had worms. The store attendant immediately took us over to the medications aisle and sold us some worm medicine. We heard your show today and thought we'd get your opinion of this.*

A: I'll bet the pet-store attendant did not ask you how much the cat weighed, what kind of symptoms of worms the cat was exhibiting, if the cat had fleas or not, if the cat was healthy or not, if the cat was on any other medications that could cause a complication and if the cat has ever been treated for this problem before and I could go on. . . .

I am not in favor of pet stores selling medications. First of all, they do not have access to the latest veterinary drugs and medications. These products are strictly controlled by FDA and the pharmaceutical manufacturers. Many times what pet stores can sell are older preparations that no longer have much demand by veterinarians.

Pet-store sales people aren't qualified to give you recommended use, dosage, side effects and so on. That's what your veterinarian is for. At times, pet-store staff may give very wrong, very dangerous information. I actually had a girl working in a pet store tell me not to put a flea collar on my cat because "cats have a hormone and therefore, the flea collar can kill them." She said it with such conviction she would have made a believer out of someone who didn't know any better.

My best advice to you is to ask your veterinarian. If he or she says something is effective and can be purchased in a pet store, then certainly buy it there to save some money. I strongly support pet stores and the role they play in helping us get good food and supplies at good prices, but they are not qualified to give medical advice.

Q: *My daddy used to pour motor oil down our barn cats' backs to keep them rid of fleas. Is that OK?*

A: What a bunch of messy barn cats you must have had. I'll bet the white ones looked like albino skunks. No, it's not OK. Motor oil contains many ingredients that will irritate the skin, as well as other compounds that could make cats very sick after being absorbed through the skin.

I've heard of people putting various things on cats' skin to treat for fleas, mites, lice and so forth. A cat's skin is thin and somewhat delicate. These types of compounds are irritating and are absorbed through the skin readily. This causes irritated skin and probably liver and kidney disease if used several times.

REAL FLEA CONTROL—THE FOUR-STEP PROCESS

Q: *Could you go over what you think is an effective flea-control program, that is safe for cats, and that we can do at home?*

A: Did you know that over one billion dollars is spent every year by pet owners trying to get rid of fleas? Flea bite dermatitis is the number one allergic skin disorder in cats and accounts for over 35% of all veterinary work in the United States!

Remember, a flea problem is an environment problem. For every adult flea you see, you have literally thousands of immature stages of the flea's life cycle in your carpet, furniture, cracks and crevices. Traditional flea-control measures, and even many of the tried and true old wives' tales, concentrate on killing the adult flea and have no effect on the many other life stages.

If you only concentrate your flea-control methods on killing the adults, you will *never* get rid of fleas. For every adult you kill, there are hundreds of eggs, larvae, pupae and young fleas (called pre-adults) waiting for the chance to be the next in line.

You must understand the stages of the flea's life cycle and the timing and environmental factors that affect this life cycle as well as the products that control each level of this life cycle before you can effectively control fleas.

It helps if you can do these things yourself because even a professional pest-control operator, who may have properly applied chemical in your pet's environment, cannot be there to treat your house every time a new flea hops in. You are there, to constantly stand vigil against these pervasive pests and that's the way you get a handle on the flea problem. It's not that hard, it just takes a little knowledge, a few trips to the pet store or animal clinic and persistence.

It takes just a quick look at the flea's life cycle to see why control must be on several levels. The four stages of a flea's life cycle are: egg, larvae, pupae, adult.

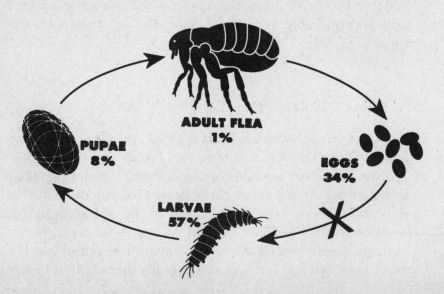

ADULT FLEA
1%

PUPAE
8%

EGGS
34%

LARVAE
57%

It may be easier to think of this life cycle as a pyramid with one adult flea at the top of the pyramid, ten to twenty pupae on the next level, fifty to sixty larvae one step below, and finally hundreds of eggs at the base.

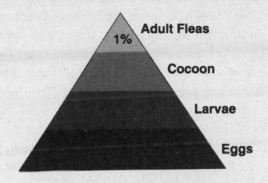

By looking at this pyramid, it's easy to see why killing adult fleas only is *not* flea control.

STEP 1: TREATING THE INDOOR ENVIRONMENT

Vacuum—The battle begins with a very thorough vacuuming. Use the crack and crevice tool and get in all the corners. Even vacuum hardwood and tile floors. Be sure to immediately throw the vacuum bag away. It will contain thousands of flea eggs, larvae and pupae that may hatch and reinfest your home. (Some people have recommended putting a piece of leftover flea collar in the vacuum bag. I do not recommend this, as the air rushing out the exhaust will contain too much chemical and some sensitive people and pets can become ill.)

Fog—Next cover your aquarium, turn your air conditioner off, ceiling fans off, turn couch pillows up on end, take the bird and the cat to Grandma's, send Rover to the neighbor's and you and the kids go see a movie! Be sure to buy enough foggers for your size home. Usually there will be some information on the side label of the fogger that will help you determine how many you need. If you have any questions, ask your veterinarian! You do not want to underdo it!

Point the fogger away from you and set it off. Carefully set the fogger on the floor in the middle of the room and get out. One by one set them off and exit the room.

You may want to spot-treat a few areas where the fog can't reach, where your pet sleeps or other heavy pet activity areas. For this purpose, you can find "premise sprays" that are like foggers but allow you to point the fogger can down and spot-treat areas.

Many foggers contain only an adulticide (agent that kills adult fleas). This means they will *only* kill adult fleas. Pre-adults, larvae, pupae and eggs are not affected. Look for foggers that also contain an insect growth regulator (IGR). This nontoxic compound works at the larvae level and prevents development of one stage to another. It is safe and has a residual effect. The IGR will prevent developing immature stages of fleas in your carpet for up to 210 days! However, adult fleas can develop from dormant pre-adults or they can catch a piggyback ride into your house on you or your pets and reinfest your home a few weeks later.

Therefore, you do not have to reapply the IGR-containing foggers each time you fog. I suggest you apply the IGR's twice a year (spring and fall). In between times, when you are seeing adult fleas, simply use an adulticide-only fogger.

Some people report a worse flea problem after using the IGR foggers. This is due to something called population dynamics. Somehow a population of fleas "knows" its been hit hard. All the pre-adult fleas that have been dormant will "sense" this and suddenly emerge (they were not affected by the adulticide or the IGR). When they emerge they are hungry and their only goal in life is to get a blood meal (from you or your pet) and then begin reproducing. Don't worry about this. It only occurs in severe infestation problems, and if it happens, simply refog your house with adulticide-only foggers about two weeks from the first fogging.

STEP 2: TREATING THE OUTDOOR ENVIRONMENT

Mow and Edge—Mow and edge the yard very well. Fleas and ticks love tall grass. It is the perfect breeding ground and serves as a constant source of reinfestation for your environment.

Spray—Once you have a neat yard, use a yard-and-kennel-type spray and follow the label directions exactly! Some sprays require you to wet the lawn first, then apply the chemical, then wet the lawn again. Others need to be applied with a special applicator on a special setting. These chemicals are safe but many of them are still toxic chemicals, so read carefully and don't use the product in any other way. Dursban is still the chemical of choice, although that changes from time to time. Your veterinarian will know the chemical your area has the best luck with.

When you're through, wash out your equipment very well, wash your hands and change your clothes if they have become wet in the process. Keep your pets off the lawn for about twenty-four hours or at least until it has dried. Take care in how you dispose of the leftover bottles and cartons. You do not want pets or kids getting into these containers.

Although this is currently under study, unfortunately there are no IGRs for outdoor use now. Sunlight breaks down the delicate compound very quickly. Therefore, you will have to spray your yard as I've described every three or four weeks, depending on the extent of your flea problem. New technology uses beneficial nematodes to eat flea larvae and pupae in your yard. See the last question in this chapter.

STEP 3: TREATING THE CAT

There are literally hundreds of products with which to bathe, dip, powder, spray, comb and brush fleas away. Some work better than others. It is impossible for me to recommend the exact product for your situation. I can, however, recommend you buy carefully. Purchase well-recognized brands and only products designed for cats. Again, the best place for advice on this is your pet's doctor.

Cats are special because of their extra sensitivity to flea chemicals. Some cats have a dermatological reaction to normal flea chemicals. Others, like the Persian, cannot tolerate some chemicals and can have a serious, even life-threatening, reaction to flea sprays and dips.

Consequently, you must make sure the chemicals you use on your cat say on the label that they are approved for use on cats. Then, use chemicals on cats in light concentrations, and sparingly, to prevent a reaction that you cannot reverse later on. As you find chemicals that are effective in getting rid of fleas, and that your cat can tolerate, then you'll feel safe about using them in the future and, if needed, in higher concentrations.

Bath and Dip—Begin with a good bath. Most cats *hate* a bath, but if you have a flea problem, you're going to have to convince the cat to tolerate this indignity every month or so during flea season. Do your best to make a bath positive and fun and quick! (See Chapter 8 for tips on bathing your cat.)

Use a mild pet shampoo that contains some flea-killing or flea-repelling ingredients. Such common and safe ingredients are pyrethrums and d-limonene. In the case of a mild flea infestation, this may be all that is needed. With kittens, this is all I recommend.

In the case of moderate or severe infestations, you will now need to dip your cat. Again using a dip designed specifically for cats or kittens, sponge the dilute chemical on the wet pet. Let the chemical stand on them for just a few minutes, then gently pat dry with a towel. Let the pet air dry the rest of the way. Unlike dipping dogs, you do want to get excess chemical off the cat. This is because they will head off to a corner and groom their wet, chemical soaked fur. Therefore, get most of it off before you let them air dry.

Flea Collars—I do recommend flea collars! Get one approved for kittens or cats and open the package and let it air out for several days before putting it on your cat. This allows the initial high concentration of chemical to dissipate a little.

Many people think flea collars don't work. In my opinion, these collars have been given a bad rap because too many people buy a flea collar only, put it on the pet and expect to never see a flea again. You can see from our discussion of the flea's life cycle that this will not work! Flea collars are well designed, researched and tested. They are effective when used as a part of this overall flea-control program. Please include it in your arsenal!

Some special flea collars now contain IGR compounds, which

is a real plus. Flea eggs that contact the collar will be unable to hatch, and in this way you are treating the environment by decreasing the viable flea-egg count in your carpet.

Even though some flea collars claim to be effective for six or more months, I've found they begin to lose effectiveness long before that. If your flea problem is a bad one, put a new collar on every three to four months.

On-Pet Sprays—Use sprays on your pet on an as needed basis. For example, when you see a flea and it is between bath times, give your cat a few sprays of a mild pet spray. Some pet sprays now contain Precor, an IGR. These work by coating the flea eggs which are laid on the cat with the IGR. This kills the egg and, therefore, stops the life cycle of the flea at the very beginning. IGRs are nontoxic and are very safe. This is why I especially recommend them for cats.

Don't overdo spraying and don't rely on spray alone, just as you should not rely on flea collars alone. *Do not* soak your cat with these sprays. Remember a few years back when Hartz Mountain released Blockade? The reason they voluntarily pulled the product after several dogs and cats died was not because the product was dangerous. It was because people were literally soaking their pets in the stuff! Hartz simply rereleased the product the next season with a string-attached instruction booklet cautioning users on its proper application. To my knowledge, there have been no more reports of problems.

STEP 1: PREVENTION

After you have done a good job of killing adult fleas and have applied the IGRs in your home, have mowed and sprayed your yard and have bathed and dipped your cat, you need to undertake a few preventive steps.

I don't recommend dusting the cat's sleeping area with flea powder. This powder will find its way into your cat's system and may cause him to cough or vomit excessively after you've done this. Instead, use a premise spray containing IGRs around your kitty's favorite sleeping places, to concentrate safe amounts of chemical in the spot.

Prevention can also involve the use of sodium borate compounds in the carpet. These naturally occurring chemicals are safe for children and pets and last in your carpet for almost a year! They are dusted on, brushed in and do not leave a residue. They work at the larval stage, much like the IGRs, and I recommend their use for people sensitive to chemicals or for those not wanting to use any toxic chemicals in the house.

Other Tricks—One of the organic gardening tricks to control fleas does have merit. Diatomaceous earth, or DE, is mother nature's insecticide. It is made up of microscopic razorlike particles that, when an insect comes in contact with them, cause its protective waxy coating to be damaged, which causes the insect to dehydrate and die. It is approved by the USDA as an ingredient in animal feeds for insect control and is very safe as long as you take precautions not to breath it in.

Do not put DE on your cat! Buy the kind of DE used in organic gardening (rather than the type used in swimming-pool filters) and apply it as a dust all over your yard about once every couple of weeks. The type of DE used in swimming pools has no insecticidal activity.

One day while driving along I was listening to a famous organic gardening expert on talk radio give some glowing testimonies about DE. He said you must be careful not to overdo it in a broadcast application because it can actually knock out all your friendly insects. Good point! Also when DE is wet it has no effect because, again, those little razor edges aren't going to have their effect of cutting the waxy coating all insects have. However, when it dries out, it becomes effective again. Therefore if you were using DE on a fire-ant mound, for example, you would not want to water it in.

In summary, this is the most concise, complete and no-nonsense approach to flea control you'll find. *Get hopping!*

> *Did You Know?*
> • The average life span of an adult flea is about 6 weeks.
> • An untreated pet can support a colony of 60 to 100 fleas.

- A female flea lays an average of 20 eggs per day—that's nearly 900 eggs in 6 weeks.
- If your pet is home to 60 fleas, they could yield 54,000 eggs in just 6 weeks.

Q: *We have recently heard about spraying "bugs" in your yard for flea control. What's that all about?*

A: In the past we have had only strong chemicals to spray in the yard to control fleas there. Unfortunately, IGR's don't work in sunlight. However, now there is an environmentally safe and effective flea fighter that goes after fleas in the yard.

Microscopic flea-eating nematodes, which are beneficial bugs, can be sprayed around your yard. This product immediately goes to work by seeking out flea larvae and destroying them. They don't harm people, pets or beneficial insects. Children and pets can play in a yard that's just been sprayed. One application works for up to four weeks.

After all the fleas are gone, the nematodes die off and biodegrade. This product is the latest thing and is now commercially available from feed stores and pet stores.

University studies have shown a 100% mortality of immature fleas after this application. It is a great idea that works well, and I recommend it.

CHAPTER 15

Ticks, Mange, Mites and Worms

"The other day we found a tick on our kitty, Sam. We were shocked! We had no idea cats got ticks!"

I've always found it interesting when I tell someone their cat is diabetic and their automatic reaction is "I didn't know cats got diabetes!" The fact is they have a pancreas just like dogs and people and that organ can stop producing insulin just like "the real thing." So I find it equally curious that people are shocked when they find a tick on their kitty. I think mostly this has to do with the fact that cats don't, or shouldn't, have as much access to the outdoors as dogs do. They are more of an inside pet and therefore their exposure is less. However, they have blood and they attract ticks and therefore they get them. They also get several associated diseases related to ticks.

Now everyone knows that cats get ear mites. Did you know that the ear mite is a cousin of the tick? Ear mites are very common in cats and sometimes very hard to get rid of. They can cause substantial damage to the ear if left untreated.

Q: *Our vet told us our two cats had ear mites about a month ago. We've treated both of them for two weeks and we still have ear mites!*

A: You have to use these medications exactly by label instructions or all the mites will not be killed and the infestation will return. If you have any other cats in the house, or if your cats visit other cats in the neighborhood, you will have a real bat-tlc on your hands, because the mites are contagious and are passed back and forth.

The most common complaint I hear about getting rid of ear mites in cats is that they "have returned." Just like treating a flea infestation, you need to know a little about their life cycle in order to effectively kill an ear-mite population.

Adult mites are the culprits of the irritation caused to the sensitive ear tissues. They are easily killed with oily substances mixed with a little insecticide, like Cerumite. However, that preparation does nothing to the nymphs that are also present in the ear canal. In a short time of only ten days, these nymphs grow to become another whole population of adult mites and begin the irritation all over again. Therefore with any ear-mite preparation you must treat for seven days, wait about seven to ten days, then retreat again for seven days. Only then will you kill the two levels—that is, adult mites and their reinforcements.

I've seen over-the-counter ear-mite treatments that do not explain this crucial treatment schedule. All veterinary prescription drugs explain this on the label and the doctor should go over this important life cycle and treatment schedule with you. You should also go in for followup checks after the medicine is gone!

Q: *I remember when my mother would put some just regular cooking oil in our cats' ears to get rid of ear mites. Does that really work?*

A: Yes, just about any oily substance will kill ear mites. The oil covers their little air-breathing holes and suffocates them. You would have to put it in on a regular basis, and for about three weeks, to kill all of the life stages, but that and mineral oil was used successfully years ago to treat this problem.

However, today you can buy a small bottle of Tresaderm or Cerumite at the animal hospital. These medications have a gentle oil-base mixed with a mild insecticide. This will take care of ear mites in short order. Tresaderm has a mild steroid in it, which will help keep the inflammation down and allow the delicate inner ear tissues to heal faster.

Q: *It must be a bad year for ticks because both our dogs, our house cat and even I have had a tick. Can you help with some advice on controlling these things?*

A: Ticks seem to be a seasonal and even regional problem. Certain tick species are in different parts of the country, but I have even seen neighborhoods with ticks and a few blocks away they've never seen one. So ticks are where you find them. They do require diligent application of chemicals in your environment on a regular basis to get rid of.

If your problem is noticeable, then you have to consider it mild to moderate. I have seen cats covered in ticks and that is severe. Just as with fleas you have to treat the pet, the yard and if your problem is severe, even the house. Luckily, ticks generally stay in the yard or on your pet. Occasionally, if the population is high and your pet is infested, they will become a problem in the house.

Just about all the chemicals and application methods used with fleas apply to ticks. There are no insect growth regulators (IGRs) for ticks, however, consequently your control will be based strictly on the adults. Their life cycle is slower in development and therefore you can get good control by controlling the adults as they emerge and become a problem.

I like to use chemicals with more of a residual effect for ticks. Diazinon granules sprinkled in the yard work well. Years ago many people used Sevin dust. However, most now report it has lost most of its effectiveness. Dursban also kills ticks, is less toxic than diazinon but is not put up in the long-acting formulas like other chemicals. If you live near a grassy or wooded area, your problem will be more intense because these are perfect breeding grounds for ticks. If you can, cut all tall grass in a twenty-foot-wide swath around your property. Treat with your chemicals into that area.

Be sure to check yourself, your dog and your cat whenever any of you have been outside. Some ticks, like the deer tick, are very small and very hard to see, so look well. Others are larger and are obvious.

For the kitty I would recommend a regular bath and dip with a mild flea and tick shampoo, and a dip chemical diluted properly for cats. Some cats don't respond well to organophosphate insecticides, so use them sparingly and quickly. Pat the cat dry and keep an eye on her as she dries off. If you insist on letting the cat outside, put an approved flea and tick collar on her. These do work if you have bathed, dipped and sprayed the yard area.

Q: *What do I do when I find a tick on my cat? Is it OK to pull it off?*
A: It is OK to pull the tick off; just do it correctly. Get a pair of tweezers and gently and steadily pull on the tick. Don't jerk it out! This gives you the best chance he will release his mouth parts and come all the way out. I suggest you place removed ticks in a jar with a small amount of dilute dip chemical in it to kill the ticks.

Don't use your hands or a tissue because you can actually inject some of the tick's contents back into your pet this way. If it were carrying a disease, you could increase your chances of transmission that way, not to mention getting infective material on your hands. Put a little alcohol on the spot, and then wash your hands.

If you do break off mouth parts in your cat's skin it will only cause a mild irritation for a while. Some of these can become more severely inflamed and make a real red and sore spot. You can use some topical ointment to help in these cases.

I would then keep an eye on the tick bite area for about a week. If the tick transmitted a disease, the area may become inflamed and this would be your signal to see the doctor.

Q: *I've always heard that heat would make a tick back out. I've seen my father blow out a match and make them back out.*
A: I suppose if you were really good and your cat were really steady, this would work, but I do not recommend it because somebody is liable to get burned in the process. If you don't want to use tweezers and pull the tick out carefully, just use a little bit of dilute dip chemical on a cotton swab and treat the tick individually. It will either back out then, or in a few days. It may even die in place and can then easily be removed with tweezers or brushing.

Q: *We've heard a lot about Lyme disease in people. You never hear about Lyme disease in cats. Do they get it?*

A: Yes, cats get Lyme disease just like you and I do, and the symptoms and secondary complications are the same. But because dogs are more commonly exposed to tick-infested areas than cats we don't hear much about it in cats. I have never seen a case of Lyme disease in a cat.

If a cat were infected, the disease would progress pretty much like it does in dogs. They would run a fever, be lethargic and may even act like it hurts to walk. Most veterinarians see dogs with Lyme disease because the owner complains of the dog being lame or simply reluctant to move. Vigorous antibiotic and supportive therapy is needed to keep dogs from having more serious complications. I would treat a cat the same way.

If you take your cat traveling into tick-infested areas, or if your cat roams tick areas around your house, I suggest you look your cat over very carefully when he comes back. Check carefully between his toes, under his belly and in his flanks, behind and in his ears. Those are favorite hiding places for ticks.

There is a vaccine against Lyme disease in dogs, but it is not approved for use in cats. Therefore, if you live in an area where this has been a problem, I would undertake strict preventive measures for you and your cats.

Q: *We put a flea collar on our cat about a month ago, and now he has a terrible rash all over his neck and ears. He is really scratching at it. The weird thing is that it has spread to our other cat. What's going on?*

A: It does not sound like a reaction to a flea collar to me. However, what you are describing could easily be notoedric mange or feline scabies. This is a very contagious form of mange in cats, and I've seen it affect whole litters and spread to the queen and to older cats. Because of the intense itching caused by the mites burrowing in the skin, these cats really produce some serious secondary skin damage. The distribution of the rash is typically around the head and neck and consistently on the ear tips.

Your veterinarian can do a skin scraping of the area and check under the microscope to see if the little mites are present. If so, be forewarned that you cannot use typical mange or mite chemicals because cats are so sensitive to these compounds. This disease is treated by first using warm soapy water soaks to loosen the scales and skin debris. Then a 2% solution of lime–sulfur solution is applied and allowed to dry. This will have to be repeated in about two weeks. All cats will have to be treated because of the highly contagious nature of this mange mite.

Q: *Our cat has been missing for a week. Thank God he came home just this morning, but, Dr. Jim, he has hundreds of tiny little seed ticks all over him. What do we do?*

A: You'll have to dip him, but I would recommend having your veterinarian do it because he will have to use a strong chemical and the doctor will want to monitor the cat after the dip. You can do this yourself, but I think it would be easier on you and the cat if a veterinarian did the work. After a day or two when you know your cat has done okay with the dip process and after all the ticks have died and let loose, you can give him a thorough and gentle grooming which will help you get most of the dead ticks out of his fur. Then a normal amount of fur care and grooming over the next few weeks should get him back to normal.

Do your best to keep this little guy in the house from now on!

PART V

NUTRITION
AND EXERCISE

CHAPTER 16

Cat Foods, Obesity and Exercise

"We've finally decided Homer is too fat!"
"What made you decide that?"
"I went to get him off the couch the other day and I had to get my wife to help me move him. He's going on a diet today. How do we do it?"

For years the leading killers of our pets were heart disease, liver disease and cancer, the top three diseases caused by poor nutrition. I think it's safe to say that for years our pet foods were killing our pets.

The pet-food business has changed dramatically in the last decade. Increased competition has made everyone do a better job of formulating their foods and educating their customers. The trend in improvement was initiated by Dr. Mark Morris who developed Hill's Pet Foods in the 1970s. Hill's began selling very high-quality foods through veterinary offices. As Hill's began educating veterinary clients about nutrition and diseases caused by poor nutrition, more and more people bought their food.

Today we have many companies such as Iams, Nature's Recipe, Natural Life, Fromm, Protocol, Nutro and many others which all make a superior pet food, back it up with lots of research and sell it through pet stores and veterinary clinics.

Superior pet-food brands now account for about 20% of pet-food sales. Ten years ago specialty brands were less than 5%! So far supermarket sales of the standard brands is down 10% in the last ten years. Because of this erosion of grocery-brand pet-food

153

sales, the major grocery-store brands such as Purina, Kal Kan and Quaker have undergone some serious reformulating. Every one of them has now created premium brands of their own. Good for them! It's about time. I believe that our pets will live longer and healthier because of this trend, and now you have a choice. It is no longer a choice between quality food for $45 dollars a bag or poor-quality grocery-store food. You now have a range of foods to choose from that allow you to spend a little more and get better nutrition for your pet at either the pet store or grocery store.

Obesity is the number one nutritional disease in American pets. Obese pets are more common with owners who are middle-aged or older and who are overweight themselves.

Many owners "love their pets to death" by feeding them far too many table scrap treats. Fat cats are more prone to some serious medical problems. Obesity puts extra stress on the cat's heart, aggravates arthritis and other joint problems and increases the risk associated with surgery. Fat cats have more digestive problems, liver disease, diabetes and even dermatitis.

Q: *We listen to your show every Saturday and really take your advice to heart. However, we just can't afford to feed all our cats pet-store food. Can you recommend a grocery-store brand for our cats that will keep them healthy?*

A: I can understand how the price of the super-premium brands sold at pet stores and veterinary clinics can be out of budget, especially with a lot of cats around the house. Most young cats will do well on most any brand. They are healthy, and their organs are pretty resilient to nutritional insult in the short term.

It is their long-term health that concerns me. I would not feed a regular grocery-store brand food to any but the healthiest of pets and then only if I had to because of cost. If you cannot afford one of the super-premium brands at your veterinary clinic or pet store, then I recommend a grocery-store premium brand. These include Alpo cat food, Expert Diet and Purina Pro Plan. These products were developed to compete with the super-premium brands sold through veterinarians and pet stores. They have a much better formula and higher-quality ingredients than the regular grocery-store brands of cat food. In cats without medical problems they are fine. Any cat with bladder disease or other medical problems should be fed only the super-premium foods available through pet stores and veterinary clinics.

Q: *We have fed our cat, Julie, one of those soft, moist type foods for some time now. She likes them very much. During a visit to the vet last week, our doctor mentioned we needed to change Julie's diet, but didn't say why. What's wrong with that kind of cat food?*

A: Your veterinarian is right! Please get Julie off whatever soft, moist brand of cat food you are feeding. These foods were someone's idea of the ultimate in convenience for cat lovers. The food didn't need to be refrigerated, it didn't smell bad and could be put up in convenient little plastic pouches. However, in their zeal for convenience, these scientists did not take into account the effects of the various additives, artificial colors, preservatives and texture enhancing chemicals used in these types of foods. We now know that these foods can cause a problem with cats' red blood cells.

It may take some time to convince Julie to eat a premium diet, but change her diet immediately. I recommend one of the top pet-store brands such as Hill's, Iams or Nature's Recipe. These foods are made with only the best ingredients and very small amounts of safe or natural preservatives. This diet change will extend the life of your cat.

Q: *For years we have fed Charlie a grocery-store brand of cat food. He has just recovered from a bladder infection, and the doctor wants us to change his food to Hill's Science Diet. Do you agree?*

A: Absolutely! Any cat with a history of bladder disease should not be on a low- to medium-priced grocery-store food because the ingredients can make the bladder problem recur. This bladder disease can even lead to serious, secondary medical problems and in some cases it can be fatal.

Your veterinarian is giving you the best medical and nutritional advice. Premium diets such as Hill's prescription diets and Science Diet are of very high quality and are formulated to prevent future problems with feline bladder disease. Sometimes the best preventive medicine isn't medicine at all—it's nutrition.

Q: *We've always fed grocery-store canned food to our cats. We don't mind the smell, and the cats love it. They are both six years old now and are getting very bad breath. Should we switch to another food?*

A: The bad breath is probably due to tartar and gum disease, which are made worse by exclusively soft diets. Have a veterinarian examine their mouths and do a dental cleaning. I recommend you switch your cats to a super-premium diet from the pet store. These foods are available in both dry and canned forms. Feeding at least part of their diet as dry food will help them keep the tartar from developing on their teeth as fast.

Because of your cats' age and nutritional history, it is important to change their diet to one of a higher quality. As your cats age, their tissues are less resistant to cellular insult. By providing them the best possible nutrition, you can prevent many medical problems caused by poor nutrition and actually extend your cat's life expectancy. Ask your veterinarian what brand of super-premium cat food he recommends.

Q: *I've seen both pet-store foods and grocery-store foods that brag that they are "all natural" and "free from added preservatives." Is this really important or is it just marketing?*

A: It is mostly marketing, but there is some scientific basis in feeding a food free of preservatives. However, most of these pet food companies are playing a name game trick on you. By saying they have "no added preservatives" they are not saying there are *no* preservatives in the food. *They* don't add them, but the preservatives have already been added to the raw ingredients before being purchased by the company! Pretty tricky isn't it?

Preservatives are necessary in all pet food. If they didn't have preservatives of some kind, they would spoil on the shelf in a matter of days or even hours. Many so-called "all natural" foods use vitamin E or vitamin C as a preservative.

Some preservatives have been tagged as the cause of problems in people and pets. The goal is to find preservatives that can be used in very small amounts and cause no side effects. Today, most pet food companies use ethoxyquin which has been found to be quite safe.

Q: *I've heard ethoxyquin is dangerous for pets, yet it is in most every pet food I look at, even pet-store and veterinary brands. What do you think?*

A: The desire for an all-natural pet food has caused every preservative added to be a target of scrutiny and often unfounded accusations.

Every few years, in circles of breeders around the country, someone will have a litter with medical problems then place the blame on a compound called ethoxyquin.

This is an additive to almost all pet foods, and some human food, that helps prevent the oxidation of fats. It gives the food a longer shelf life, prevents the formation of dangerous toxins in the food, and makes the food taste better. There is even some evidence that the chemical has some anticancer properties. Gee, what more do you want from a preservative?

Ethoxyquin has been tested and retested and has been found to be safe time and time again. It has been successfully used in pet food for over thirty years. Even the "all-natural," "no-preservatives-added" foods have it, where it is added to the basic ingredients before the manufacturer formulates the food.

It is used at a level of .001 ounce per average daily ration. It prevents the use of other preservatives such as BHA and BHT which would have to be used in substantially higher amounts thus adding to the cost of pet food. The most researched and highly formulated premium brands of pet food contain this compound because of its many benefits.

There have been no scientific studies, data, trials or investigations done or cited to support the claim that ethoxyquin causes any problems.

Q: *We were in a pet store the other day to buy some cat food. The salesperson tried to get us to buy a brand we have never heard of and that is sold only by this particular pet-store chain. What do you think?*

A: Some stores sell private label brands of foods that are made by giant food manufacturers. These foods are of very average quality at best, but some stores lead their customers to believe they are a special premium brand.

The store's profit margin is much greater on this food than on the other brands, so the employees may have been instructed to encourage customers to buy it.

Stick with the name super-premium pet-store brands like Hill's, Iams and Nature's Recipe or the premium grocery brands like Purina Pro Plan, Expert and Alpo, and stay away from brands you've never heard of.

Q: *How do I know if my cat is overweight? She's a four-year-old Domestic Shorthair and weighs fifteen pounds.*

A: Most adult cats weigh eight to fourteen pounds depending on their breed. Some big breeds, like the Maine Coon, have a large skeletal frame and can weigh up to eighteen to twenty pounds and be quite normal. So, it depends on your cat's general build if fifteen pounds is overweight.

Cats should look lean and sleek. If she looks pudgy, she is probably overweight. The best method is to simply feel her ribs with your fingertips. You should be able to feel the ribs easily. If all you feel is fat, the cat is obese. If you can easily count the ribs by running your fingertips along the rib cage, your cat is probably just right.

The next time you're at the veterinary office, have your doctor give you his opinion as well.

Q: *We want to neuter our male cat, but we are afraid he will get fat. Any advice?*

A: Yes, go ahead and neuter him. Obesity exists when body weight exceeds the optimum for the pet by 15%. It is the most common nutritional disease in dogs and cats. It is more common in older pets and occurs more often in females than males— and, yes, it is more common in neutered pets. They require one-third less calories than their nonneutered friends. Simply feed him less after the neuter surgery.

Most cats like to free-choice feed, but it is usually these cats that become overweight. I suggest you feed your adult cat two times a day and carefully regulate the amount so he stays at a nice weight. Most cats should weigh between eight to ten pounds unless they are an unusually large breed. Much above that and you should begin to think about a reducing diet.

Q: *Our vet, as well as all our cat-loving friends, have told us we need to reduce Chico's weight. How do we do it?*

A: Start by making it a family rule not to give Chico treats. Everyone must be in on this program. Next you must remember that reducing weight involves two key elements: (1) reducing the amount of calories he takes in and (2) making him burn more calories than he takes in, every day.

Nature's Recipe makes a product called Optimum Feline Lite Diet that I highly recommend and Hill's Prescription Diet Feline r/d is also specifically made for reducing cats. These foods are high in indigestible fiber so that the cat feels more full when he eats. The fat and carbohydrate content is low, and this decreases overall calories. Feed about 20% less than the amount that you are used to feeding now, and feed it in two to three feedings over the day.

Once Chico is at a good weight, you should switch to a diet which will help keep the weight off. I recommend either Prescription Diet Feline w/d, or Science Diet Feline Maintenance Light, or Nature's Recipe Optimum Feline Diet Lite. These foods are excellent quality, high in fiber content, and are also low in fat and calories.

Don't forget, you will need to make an effort to exercise Chico several times a day in order for his diet to be successful.

Q: *We've tried to reduce out cat's weight, but we're not having much luck. How do you get a cat to exercise?*

A: You'll have to get creative about kitty games. Some sedentary cats are very hard to motivate. You can make a homemade cat exerciser by tying a piece of cloth or a small catnip cat toy to the end of a string and making it do flips in front of the cat. The key is to make the toy move like an insect or a real mouse. Not just any cat toy will motivate a fat cat.

Start slow and work up to several minutes of kitty aerobics every day. Overweight cats cannot play very long at first but will be able to work up gradually.

Q: *Our cat is way overweight. My mother wants to make her a home cooked reduction diet with tuna and rice. What do you think about that?*

A: I'd highly recommend against doing this. Feline nutrition is very complex and even the PhDs are still learning about all the cat's special requirements. If you cook for the cat at home, I can almost guarantee the diet will be unbalanced and deficient in something. When you are trying to reduce your cat's weight is not a time to be guessing at diet content.

By the way, tuna is fine for people but fed to cats exclusively, it can cause amino acid problems and fatty liver disease. The oil tuna is packed in adds too much fat to the diet, especially to a reduced calorie diet.

I suggest a commercial reducing diet, either a prescription diet from your veterinary office, or one of the reduced-calorie foods at the pet store.

Q: *My dad started playing with our cat, Belinda, to help her lose some weight. She plays with my dad, but after a while she breathes very hard. Is that hurting her?*

A: I would definitely be careful with this. Just as with people, you cannot take an overweight cat and suddenly start doing high-impact aerobics. Because obesity puts extra stress on the heart, lungs, liver and kidneys, overexertion could cause failure of one of these organ systems, and the results could be life threatening.

Begin by playing for just a few minutes several times a day. Over a period of a month, simply increase the amount of time or the number of times per day that she plays. After she appears to be losing weight and is healthier and more eager to play, then you can pick up the pace more.

Q: *We are trying to get Sammy's weight down and have bought special cat food for him, but now he is eating the dog's food. What do we do?*

A: Put the dog food where Sammy can't reach it! There is no doubt that Sammy is hungry, and he will even seek out dog food. Place the dog's food in another room, or perhaps feed the dog outside for a while until you can get Sammy's weight down.

CHAPTER 17

Types of Food
and Specialty Diets

*"I think my mother has gone a little nuts since living alone
with her three cats"*

"What do you mean?"

*"Every time we visit her she is fixing them some new kind
of food. She buys all different flavors of canned food and she
must have twenty partial sacks of dry food in her cupboard.
Yesterday was the clincher. We all sat down for dinner and
she came out with the three cats' meals on a platter and
announced they were having cat food with tuna and
anchovy!"*

Our pets are very special to us. Feeding our pets is one of the tangible things we can give back to them. However, everything we put inside them affects their health, their resistance to disease and their longevity.

Not a talk radio program goes by that I am not asked the question, "What type of food should I feed my pet?" There is not a simple answer because there are so many diets available. Almost 60% of cat owners buy a cat food purely by experimentation! Happily another 37% buy their cat's food based on their veterinarian's recommendation.

More and more diseases seen in veterinary practice today are being treated either primarily with nutrition or as an adjunct to traditional medical therapy. In cats, heart failure, kidney disease, liver disease, bladder disease, skeletal diseases and fractures, endocrine imbalances, obesity, allergies, skin disease, diabetes, diarrhea and even cancer are at least partially treated with nutrition.

Q: *We have a new kitten and a four-year-old cat in the house. The kitten is eating the adult cat's food. Will that hurt him?*

A: No, he's just not getting the extra nutrients he needs as a kitten. The kitten food gives him the extra protein and calcium he needs to grow up strong. Make an effort to feed them separately.

Q: *We've fed our old cat a standard grocery-store brand cat food for the last thirteen years. Should we change her food now, because of her age?*

A: I would! As your cat goes through life, many things happen. She is exposed to toxins, chemicals, residues, stress, allergens and lots of nitrogen waste products from the protein in her food. An older cat needs special nutrition to "go easy" on its kidneys, immune system and intestinal tract. Geriatric cats need the highest-quality food, made for older cats.

   Feline nutrition is critical for preventing disease, yet it was just recently that manufacturers began producing senior cat foods. These senior diets are made with more restricted, although adequate, levels of protein and phosphorous, with moderate levels of salt. They may have a slightly higher amount of fat so the cat can get its calories from fat instead of protein which can stress delicate kidney tissue. The reduced sodium will lower blood pressure and therefore decrease stress on the heart muscle.

   I recommend Hill's Science Diet Feline Senior or Nature's Recipe Optimum Feline Lite.

Q: *Our vet recommends we give our cat taurine tablets. We feed Barney Iams cat food and feel like he is in good shape. Why do we need these vitamins?*

A: First of all, taurine is an amino acid not a vitamin. A few years back it was discovered that the pet food companies, even the top premium manufacturers, were not including enough taurine in cat food. This was not their fault. In fact, most cat foods were including five to ten times the National Research

Council's recommendation, but cats were either not absorbing or not retaining the taurine.

Consequently, veterinarians saw some diseases traceable to this taurine deficiency—primarily heart problems, but vision and reproduction are also affected. Because of this, many veterinarians began to recommend taurine supplements.

However, very quickly, practically all cat food brands started to fortify with taurine and there was no longer the need to supplement. Iams cat food is certainly one of the diets that has adequate levels of taurine.

Unless your cat has some unusual taurine malabsorption problem, or a rare disease known as aminoaciduria, where the taurine is excreted in the urine without being utilized by the cat's body, you probably don't need the supplement. Remind your veterinarian that Barney is on a taurine-fortified food, and ask if he still wants the taurine supplement continued. If the answer is yes, ask why.

Q: *My cat is fed Hill's Science Diet. I am in the habit of giving her a Pet Tab every day. Is that OK?*

A: A super-premium brand like Hill's needs no supplementation unless there is a specific need. In the absence of a specific medical reason, this supplementation can actually throw off the delicate balance of nutrients provided by the formula.

Years ago, when mediocre, grocery-store brands of cat food were common, our cats needed this type of supplementation because they were not getting fresh sources of vitamins and minerals in the foods and some foods were simply not well balanced. However, that has all changed now, and supplementing a premium food may actually be doing more harm than good.

Q: *Would canned or dry food be better for our new six-month-old kitten?*

A: Technically, as long as you buy one of the premium brands it does not matter. Both forms are formulated to be the same in terms of nutrition, quality and balance. However, the canned food is mostly water and you're paying for that water on a weight basis. Dry food is by far the better bargain.

Because cats like that extra bit of flavor and smell, I do like to give my cats canned food, but not exclusively. They eat a base of dry food, then once or twice a day I'll give them a small amount of canned food. This stimulates their interest in eating and they are quite happy.

Another thing to consider is that feeding exclusively canned food will be more likely to cause dental tartar problems later in life. Dry food helps remove some tartar from the cats' teeth as they eat.

Q: *We saw a food in the grocery store that said it was "low ash." What does that mean and is that good?*

A: Many foods these days are touted as "low ash." Foods with large amounts of magnesium, phosphorous, calcium and other minerals show up as high in ash content in a laboratory analysis. Because current thinking is that low dietary magnesium, calcium and phosphorous help cats with feline urological syndrome (FUS), many manufacturers have jumped on the bandwagon with the low ash claim. This has lead many cat owners to assume that *ash is bad*.

In fact some specialty pet foods touted as low ash are *not* low in magnesium and therefore do not help in the prevention of FUS.

While it is true a diet low in magnesium, phosphorous and calcium seems to help prevent FUS, these minerals are also essential to normal health. The key to preventing FUS is a *proper restriction* in the amounts of these minerals and a food that makes the urine slightly acidic when it is excreted.

This is a perfect example of why you should buy premium brands of pet foods and stay away from the bargain brands.

Q: *I know cats are carnivores and need meat. I also know they require lots of protein, however I saw a food in the pet store the other day with 55% protein! Isn't that too much?*

A: Yes! Cats do require a higher protein level than other pets— about 30%. But many pet foods contain 50% to 60% protein! For cats with compromised kidney function, that level of protein will accelerate kidney failure and is totally unnecessary.

Q: I know cats crave milk, but my cat throws up when I give her some. Do you think she has a medical problem?

A: Most likely not, she is probably quite normal. There are many myths and old wives' tales about feeding cats. Probably the most popular is that cats crave or need milk. Some cats can tolerate milk, but they do not *need* it. Many cats cannot digest the milk sugar lactose and therefore milk gives them diarrhea or may make them throw up soon after ingesting it.

If you really want to give your cat milk, there are sources of lactose-free milk for cats. Cat Sip made by AkPharma and Dairy Cat made by Alpo are two.

Q: We've had our cat on c/d for a month after his bout with FUS. Do we have to stay on this food? It's kind of expensive, and we have to get it from the vet.

A: Very good question. Hill's Prescription Diet c/d is the diet of choice after a cat has had an episode of feline urological syndrome, or FUS. Because at least one of the causes of this disease is a high magnesium and phosphorous levels in the food the cat eats, c/d is formulated to be restricted in these and other minerals that can contribute to the disease. It also will create an acidic urine when excreted, which helps prevent the development of the crystals that form in the urine with this syndrome.

However, once a cat has not shown the typical symptoms of FUS for one to two months, I feel you can change to one of the other diets that accomplishes these same nutritional and metabolic goals. This is such a common problem and there is so much demand for these types of foods, many brands now do this. In keeping with the same manufacturer, I recommend you buy Hill's Science Diet Feline Maintenance from your pet store. It is also restricted in these minerals and creates an acid urine when excreted and the maintenance diet will be less expensive.

Q: We have been trying to figure out what is wrong with our cat for several months. Now the doctor thinks it may be a food allergy. Does that sound suspicious to you?

A: Not at all. Food allergies are more common than once thought, and true allergies to food are not easy to diagnose. Food allergy causes dermatitis, itching, vomiting and sometimes diarrhea. It is more common in dogs but can be seen in cats as well.

In order to determine if food allergy is responsible for your cat's problems, you must completely avoid feeding your pet anything he has previously been eating. Since most commercial pet foods contain approximately the same ingredients, and most pets with food allergies have been eating the same diet for some time, just changing the brand of food does not alter the symptoms.

Common ingredients that cause food allergies are beef, milk, chicken, eggs, fish, soy, wheat and corn. These are also common ingredients in many pet foods.

Many companies have come out with lamb and rice diets which they advertise as hypoallergenic. However, lamb is not necessarily hypoallergenic. Lamb can cause allergies if fed over a long period of time just like any other food ingredient. In fact, in Great Britain, where lamb is commonly fed, it is the major cause of food allergy in dogs and cats.

To determine if your cat is allergic to food, you must put her on a test diet for at least a month. For cats, this test diet is simply lamb baby food. You gradually mix small amounts of the baby food in with your cat's current diet until your cat is accustomed to the new taste. Then withdraw the old diet.

It's best to feed slightly less than your pet normally eats in a day. If your pet refuses to eat the test diet for several days, or has an upset stomach, you can go temporarily back to the old diet. After the problem subsides, you can try the test diet again. Once your cat is on the test diet, it may take up to twelve weeks for symptoms to disappear. If the cat's symptoms improve, it is likely that the problem is, in fact, a food allergy.

It is not intended for you to feed this test diet to your cat indefinitely. You simply begin introducing food ingredients one at a time, a new one about every two weeks. One by one you add back beef, milk, chicken, cooked egg, etc., until you see the symptoms recur. Then you've found the culprit.

Q: *We've been undergoing the test diet of lamb baby food to see if our cat has food allergies. Today, he got into the dog's food and ate a fair amount. Is that going to mess up our test?*

A: Yes, you basically have to start over. Even one bite of something else means you will need to start from the beginning again. Make sure you feed the dog and cat separately. Also make sure no one gives your kitty a treat of some kind during the test.

Once you have found the offending ingredient and are on a maintenance diet, you will have to be just as careful to make sure your cat doesn't eat the dog's food.

Q: *Our cat has a heart condition and among all the medications the vet has prescribed is a food that he sells at the clinic called h/d. Is this necessary?*

A: Absolutely! First let me say it sounds like your doctor is on top of things and please don't be put off by an array of medications and diet formulas. Heart disease in cats can be very serious, even life threatening, and your vet is simply doing all he can to get kitty back up to speed.

One of the problems with various forms of heart disease in both dogs and cats is high blood pressure, which causes more workload on the heart. Most cat foods are quite high in sodium, which makes this problem worse. Therefore, just as with dogs and humans, a low-salt diet is a must when treating and maintaining heart patients. In fact, many doctors have found we can control mild heart cases with low sodium diets alone!

Q: *Our big Maine Coon Cat, Bubba, has been diagnosed with DCM. The doctor seemed quite cautious and has run a battery of tests and sent us home with a great many medications, including taurine tablets. Can you fill in some of the blanks on this disease?*

A: Yes. DCM stands for dilated cardiomyopathy. It is a disease of the muscle of the heart where the cat's ventricles dilate, preventing the heart from pumping efficiently. It can be quite severe, even acutely fatal! That is why the doctor was so cautious. The fact that he has sent you home with medications tells me that the cat is not critical. I hope its chances for survival are good.

It has been known since the 1970s that taurine, an amino acid, is essential for normal function of the retina. But just recently have we discovered it is also essential for normal heart muscle. Before 1987 most cat foods had as much as fifteen times the National Research Council's recommendations for taurine, so you would think that would be more than enough. But as it turns out, cats were either not absorbing it or not retaining it in high enough concentrations and veterinarians had been seeing dilated cardiomyopathy caused by a taurine deficiency.

Now, not all cardiomyopathies are caused by taurine deficiency, but most are, and therefore your doctor has prescribed the taurine supplement. All the other medications you have are to help the cat through a very critical time in hopes that the heart muscle will rebuild. You should keep this cat as still as possible for the first ten days. If he makes it through that critical period, the chances for his long-term survival are quite good.

Currently most high-quality-pet-food manufacturers have doubled again the amount of taurine in their foods, and tests have shown that this will maintain adequate blood levels to prevent DCM.

Q: *We have an eleven-year-old alley cat that is going downhill fast. The doctor has diagnosed kidney problems and prescribed medications and a special diet. What are our chances?*

A: Kidney disease in middle-aged to older cats is all too common. It has various causes, not the least of which is poor nutrition when the kitty was young. Now, however, it is special nutrition that will be his biggest saving grace. There are no specific medications to treat kidney disease, only ones that help with secondary complications. The kidney has precious little capacity to heal itself, but it can if given the chance.

That is why your veterinarian has prescribed a special diet, called k/d. This food has restricted amounts of very high-quality protein. The object is to reduce the amount of nitrogenous wastes and phosphorous the kidney has to deal with so that it can heal.

You see, poor-quality foods contain proteins that create a great deal of these waste products and bit by bit they take their toll on those delicate nephrons in the kidney. If your cat has gone down fast, the prognosis will have to be guarded. Good luck.

Many people lose their beautiful, long-time family cats to renal failure every year. If cat lovers realized that behind all the cutesy advertising and brand names of average, grocery-store cat food was this insidious destruction of delicate kidney tissues, they would be outraged. Cat owners need to know that high-quality nutrition for the entire lifetime of the cat would allow them to keep these little guys around longer.

PART VI

MEDICINE AND DISEASE

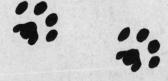

CHAPTER 18

The Alphabet Soup
of Cat Diseases

"Let's go to Mary in Columbia, South Carolina. Hi Mary."

*"Dr. Jim, I have three cats, two of them are outside cats
and one is a house cat . . . they were all very healthy until
one got PIF . . . I'd never heard of PIF until the doctor told
me my cat had it and that there was no cure . . . he also told
me my other cats could get it and . . . I should watch them
very carefully . . . my cat was looking just fine and I feed it
very good food . . . my mother has a cat from this litter and it
is fine . . . I don't understand why this one cat would get this
disease. . . ."*

"Mary! . . . "

"Yes?"

"Do you have a question for me?"

"Oh, yes. Do you know anything about this PIF disease?"

"You mean F, I, P?"

"Yeah. That's it!"

Feline diseases are literally an alphabet soup of acronyms. If you
are confused about them, you're not alone. Most people find this
list a bit confusing. Many feline diseases have similar causes and
symptoms. It takes time and experience to differentiate between
them.

If you hadn't had a cat in many years and took a new little kitty
into a veterinary hospital for its initial evaluation and vaccinations, it could be a little overwhelming. In the past decade we
have developed vaccines for many deadly viruses that attack cats,

including the leading killer of cats in the world—feline leukemia. In fact, this was the first vaccine ever known to prevent cancer.

There are now vaccines against feline infectious peritonitis, or FIP, a disease that has baffled scientists for three decades. We can vaccinate our cats against rhinotrachitis, calicivirus and pan-leukopenia. I suspect that a vaccine for feline AIDS, or FIV (feline immunodeficiency virus), is not far away.

Q: I heard cats can get AIDS, is that true?
A: No, cats cannot get human AIDS. There is a virus that causes an AIDS-like illness in cats, but it is transmittable only from cat to cat.

Feline immunodeficiency virus (FIV) was first identified in 1986 in a California cattery where they were seeing chronic and recurring infections. The disease has been referred to as feline AIDS because the acquired immunodeficiency syndrome that occurs is in many ways similar to HIV.

Outdoor, free-roaming cats are at the greatest risk of getting FIV. The positive FIV rate is three times higher in males than females with the most common age being five to six years. The higher incidence in males is probably due to territorial fighting, since the virus is transmitted mostly by cat-fight wounds. Casual contact through eating out of the same dish and simply living together does not seem to pose a particular risk.

FIV occurs four to six weeks after an infection with the virus. It develops in three stages. The acute stage is seen initially and lasts for about three weeks. These cats have a fever and will show positive for FIV on a blood test.

During the second stage, cats have a latent period that can last months or years. These cats also test FIV positive when checked.

The third, chronic or terminal, stage of the disease may last for a few weeks to a few months. We see many symptoms related to the immunodeficiency at this time. Opportunistic infections, tumors and neurological signs are common. Many of these cats come into the clinic with infections in their mouths or with nonhealing abscesses. Curiously, some of these cats will test FIV negative. They look just like cats with chronic feline leukemia (FeLV), with the varying symptoms.

Currently there is no effective treatment for FIV. We can only support the cat with appropriate antibiotics, antifungals and nutrition. Most cats die within six months to three years after entering the chronic third stage. Any FIV-positive cat should be strictly confined indoors to lessen his risk of getting infections and to prevent his spreading the disease to other cats.

Q: *Our vet told us about a new disease our cat should be vaccinated against, called peritonitis. Is that vaccine necessary?*

A: I think so. Feline infectious peritonitis, or FIP, is more common than we once thought. For the past three decades, veterinarians have had to tell cat owners with FIP-positive cats there was little hope. Just recently do we have a vaccine that will prevent this strange and fatal disease.

FIP is seen in a high percentage of feline-leukemia-positive cats, which leads researchers to believe it is stress related. Infection rates increase with stresses such as crowding, poor nutrition, steroid use and other viral infections. FIP is always fatal in both domestic and wild cats. We do not know how the disease is transmitted, and no effective treatment or cure for the infected cat has been developed. FIP kills 500,000 cats a year in this country.

There is not a test to distinguish FIP from other feline viruses, therefore countless numbers of cases have gone undiagnosed or misdiagnosed over the past thirty years.

Its course is lengthy and debilitating. FIP cats won't eat. They run a fever, lose weight and become anemic. Once symptoms are noticed, it's generally too late for all but trying to ease the cat's suffering.

Cats can get several forms of FIP. In the so called "wet form" there is a buildup of fluid in the cat's chest or abdomen. The "dry form" attacks the cat more slowly, and an early diagnosis is almost impossible because of the lack of observable signs. To make things even more complex, cats can also have a combination of these two forms.

This disease hits two age groups particularly hard—kittens with developing immune systems, and cats more than eleven years old, whose immune systems are weakening.

Cats most at risk include those in multicat households, purebred cats and, once again, cats allowed outdoors. The virus is spread through direct contact between cats, or from queen to kittens.

The first breakthrough in thirty years with this disease came a few years ago with the introduction of a vaccine given in the form of nose drops. This vaccine causes an effective immune response which will fight off infection once the cat is exposed. It is recommended that healthy cats sixteen weeks of age or older receive two doses, three to four weeks apart. This then becomes a part of the cat's annual immunizations.

Q: *It's been a while since we've had a cat at our house. We've heard you talking about leukemia. Is this something we need to know more about?*

A: Yes. Feline leukemia virus, or FeLV, is the leading killer of cats in the world, even big cats and exotics. The incidence of infection nationwide is about 13%. Happily, we now have an effective vaccine for this deadly disease. However, you should know that no vaccine is 100% effective. If your cat is exposed to an infected cat, it can be a serious matter. Your veterinarian may want to boost your cat's immunization.

FeLV is a virus that enters the body through the eyes, nose and mouth. Once established, it can suppress your cat's ability to make new white blood cells. The cat's white blood cells become cancerous and, therefore, not effective in fighting off infections. The disease may also cause solid tissue tumors to form. The cat may die of overwhelming infection, leukemia or cancer.

Some cats can fight off the infection. However, once a cat is permanently infected, most will die within three years.

Although the first vaccine for feline leukemia was available in 1985, eight years later FeLV is still the number one killer of cats in the world.

What is the reason? A recent survey showed 80% of cat owners are at least aware of feline leukemia, but of those 80%, only 30% were certain their cats had been immunized against it. The same study showed that cat owners would be willing to spend the $20 to $40 necessary to vaccinate their cats. So it is a matter of education and awareness.

Cats get feline leukemia through close contact with infected cats, such as mutual grooming and sharing food, water bowls and litter boxes. Therefore, as with so many risks to our cat's health, this disease is seen more in outdoor cats, or those in multicat households.

Even single, indoor cats can get the disease if they come into contact with other cats while they're boarded or if they escape outside, even once.

Your best protection against this killer is vaccination. Not all veterinarians recommend that all cats should receive this vaccine, but if you have never discussed this issue with your veterinarian, please call today and do so.

Q: *I've heard a lot about FUS. Why don't you ever mention vaccinating against that?*

A: FUS, or feline urological syndrome, is not an infectious disease caused by a bacterium or virus. Therefore we cannot vaccinate against it. It is simply the formation of mineral crystals, stones or plugs in the cat's urinary bladder and urethra, the urine tube leading to the outside of the body.

These crystals, called struvite, can many times be passed and cause little problem. However, these cats' bladders are more prone to bacterial infection. This infection adds cellular debris to the mix of crystals and plugs and may cause a blockage of the urine tube.

As you can imagine, this blockage is painful and makes it difficult for the cat to urinate. You would see a cat that visited the litter box frequently and produced only small amounts of urine, sometimes with a little blood in it.

Sometimes these cats become completely blocked and cannot urinate, even after trying for a long time. They will cry in pain, strain to urinate but cannot. This blockage occurs in both male and female cats, but because of the tiny urine tube in male cats, it is much more common in males. This is referred to as a "blocked tom" cat. If the urine tube is not cleared within a few hours, the cat may die. Therefore, this is a medical emergency where immediate action must be taken.

Cats that are prone to FUS are typically two to six years of age, overweight and neutered. They spend most of their time indoors and do not exercise. Persians seem to be particularly prone to FUS.

The only prevention is medication from your cat's doctor, diet and quick recognition of the signs of trouble. Once a cat has blocked, he may very well do it again. So always watch his urination habits.

Q: *I've got a weird one for you Doc. Our cat has got hemo bart o nell osis! Now where do you suppose he got that?*

A: Hemobartonellosis or feline infectious anemia (FIA) was actually diagnosed more commonly before we knew about FeLV. Much of what was actually FeLV-related anemia was considered FIA. Now, however, we know how to differentiate between FeLV and the blood parasite called *Hemobartonella felis*. This little parasite gets on the outside of the cat's red blood cell and damages it. These damaged blood cells are taken up by the spleen, and that causes the anemia.

Most of these cats show a positive result on a test for autoimmune disease, so many researchers think the development of the anemia may be at least partly caused by an autoimmune mechanism. In other words, the cat's own immune system sees the blood cells as foreign and destroys them.

There are several factors which seem to predispose a cat to the development of FIA. FeLV, no prior vaccinations, a history of cat-fight wounds, an age of less than three years and being an outdoor cat all seem to make a cat more prone. We still don't know how the parasite is transmitted from one cat to another, but it must be a blood transmission. Therefore fleas, ticks and biting flies are generally thought to be the most likely form of transmission.

FIA cats can be put on a special antibiotic which suppresses the development of the organism and allows the cat to recover. It will take about thirty days of treatment. However, even then the cat is not completely rid of the blood parasite, since many of the treated cats become carriers of the disease.

Q: *I heard on a news report that there is a real problem with rabies in cats. Is that true?*

A: As a matter of fact, Yes! Interestingly, over the past few years there has been an increasing number of rabies cases in cats. The northeastern United States and the Mexican border states have serious trouble with rabies every year, but we are seeing a statistical rise of cases in cats.

The reason may be because of stray cats and the fact that the cat population is less protected because cats don't see the veterinarian as much, and therefore, don't get the rabies vaccine as often, as do dogs.

Please do not let your cat's rabies vaccination lapse. This is a very serious disease that is successfully and inexpensively prevented.

Q: *Why do we have to vaccinate cats? I thought they got protection from their mother's milk. Besides, what did they do when man wasn't around to give them these shots?*

A: My guess is that many more cats died before man was around to vaccinate them. Secondly, we have created quite an artificial environment for these animals and, therefore, they are exposed to many more pathogens and other disease-causing agents than in a natural world.

Kittens are provided with some immunity to many of these feline diseases from their mother. Mother's antibodies are transmitted to the kittens through the placenta, the birth sac. These antibodies, called maternal antibodies, enter the kitten's circulation at a very early age and can only protect the kitten from diseases for which the mother herself has protection. In fact, this is the reason we often recommend boosting the mother's immunity a few months before breeding.

While it is true that mother nature has made this system work quite well to protect kittens from disease, the immunity lasts only a few weeks. This leaves the kitten susceptible to disease during early growth phases. Thus, many unprotected kittens die before reaching four to six months of age because they come into contact with a disease for which they have no protection.

Q: *When do we start vaccinations for our cat? We have heard various times, from four weeks to ten weeks. What is best?*

A: I think a vaccination program for kittens should begin at six to eight weeks of age depending on the general health of both the kitten and its mother. Most veterinarians recommend a vaccine that includes rhinotrachitis, calicivirus and panleukopenia.

All cats that will have exposure to outdoor cats also need leukemia and FIP vaccines. Other high-risk cats need these vaccines also, such as those who are boarded or on the show circuit.

Q: *Our vet recommended we vaccinate our cat for parvovirus. I've heard of this in dogs—but cats?*

A: Yes, parvovirus in cats is quite common, but we usually don't refer to it as such. It is the feline panleukopenia virus, also known as "PanLeuk" or even feline enteritis. It is a vaccine that is automatically included in the kitten and annual shots your veterinarians gives. I'm surprised he refereed to it in that fashion.

Q: *Our cat got a serious cold and respiratory infection. I thought that was a part of the vaccinations he received each year?*

A: There are several infectious diseases that cause a respiratory infection that we vaccinate for every year. However, there are a whole array of agents that cause respiratory infections in cats for which we have no vaccine.

Rhinotrachitis and calicivirus are the two most common preventable feline upper-respiratory diseases. Many veterinarians routinely vaccinate against these. However, a respiratory disease can be caused by many viruses, bacteria and even chlamydial organisms.

Q: *Our cat never goes outside. Yet every three years, like clockwork, our veterinarian recommends we get the rabies vaccine. Is that really necessary in my case?*

A: From a practical standpoint, the likelihood your cat will be exposed to a rabid animal, and therefore, come in contact with the rabies virus is unlikely. However, there is always a very slight chance, and because rabies is often fatal in both animals and people, we usually take no chances. Most veterinarians vaccinate according to their state's laws.

That brings up another point. It is a law that your pet be vaccinated against rabies. In fact, many states have a more stringent law and require the vaccine every year! These are usually Mexican border states, and states with a persistent problem with rabies outbreaks.

We are seeing more rabies in cats than ever before, and I believe that this is in part because cat owners typically don't see their veterinarian as often as do dog owners and are more lax about preventive medicine. There have been several outbreaks of the rabies virus in the Northeast in recent years, and many people have been exposed.

Take my advice, get the rabies vaccine as often as your veterinarian recommends. It is very inexpensive insurance for you and your cat.

Q: *Our cat was recently vaccinated for all the kitty diseases. About two hours after we brought him home he began to breath very fast and act very uncomfortable. Finally he broke out with a rash on his belly and we took him back to the vet. Our vet said it was a vaccine reaction and kept him overnight. Is that common?*

A: No, that is quite rare. Cats do very well after vaccination. Most of the vaccine agents are well tested and create little problem. However, there are no absolutes. I have seen cats have vaccine reactions. Most of the time the reaction is respiratory distress and rapid breathing.

If you should see a different veterinarian in future years, be sure to tell that doctor that your cat had this reaction so he can premedicate the cat to help prevent some of the reaction. It is not usually advisable to stop vaccinating the cat, because that would put it at even greater risk.

Q: *We had our cats vaccinated for leukemia last year. Today we've learned that our oldest one, Kay, has leukemia. Why didn't the vaccine prevent this disease?*

A: Vaccines are not 100% protection. We are "asking" the cat's immune system to produce enough of an antigen–antibody response to build immunity, but not actually cause disease. Usually this works. However, sometimes a cat's system can be overwhelmed by a very "hot" virus or a very big dose of virus.

Also, its immune system, which was once working quite well, could now have failed for some reason. In addition, individual cats vary in their susceptibility to disease.

The case of feline leukemia virus (FeLV) is very strange and complicated. Some cats may be positive on one test, and negative on another. Some may be negative and convert to positive due to stress. Even the manufacturer of the leading FeLV vaccine says their vaccine is only 80% effective. It is the best thing we have for preventing this disease, and we hope it works. There are cases like yours, however, where it doesn't.

Q: *We took our cats in for FeLV vaccinations today and the vet wouldn't give them until he tested the cats first. Why is that?*

A: Vaccinating FeLV-positive cats, while it won't hurt them, won't help them either. Plus, if any of your cats are positive, you need to know that so you can watch them more closely, have more frequent checkups and isolate them from new arrivals. Studies show that 3% to 5% of the general cat population test positive to FeLV. Almost half of all sick cats are found to be positive.

One FeLV-positive test is not the "end of it all" either. A positive ELISA test means the cat has either an early infection, a latent infection or a permanent infection. Therefore after a positive ELISA, I always retest cats three months later. If the test is negative at that time, that means the cat overcame the infection (which is what mother nature wants them to do) and is no longer positive. Forty percent of all cats do this. Another 30% become latent carriers and the remaining 40% become persistently infected and will die within three months to three years.

We also usually run an IFA test. This test checks for the virus in the bloodstream, while the ELISA test checks for the presence of the virus in the lymphatic system. The IFA test can tell us how the cat is handling the infection. If it comes back negative, there is a good likelihood the cat will overcome the infection. Another IFA is run three months later and if it is again negative, it means we are in the clear. If positive at that time, it means the virus got the upper hand on the cat's ability to overcome the infection.

Q: *A friend of mine is a vet technician, and she said there was some concern about the feline leukemia virus being transmitted to people. Is that true?*

A: This has been looked at carefully, especially by researchers who work with this virus extensively. There has never been a case of antibodies to the FeLV virus in either research workers or cancer patients. FeLV is a species-specific virus (as are most viruses) and therefore is not likely to infect humans. Long-term statistics show the incidence of cancer in people with cats and without cats to be the same. So I would not worry about it.

CHAPTER 19

Cancer

*"Dr. Jim, we've just come back from the vet and our cat has
the same thing President Reagan had (the caller said
proudly)—skin cancer!"*

Interestingly, animals are four times more likely to have cancer
than man. In cats, there is a more serious statistic—cats' tumors
are much more likely to be malignant than those in dogs. The
incidence of tumors in cats is about 300 per 100,000 cats, and the
tumors are more likely to involve the skin and blood system.

The best thing we can do for cancer, whether in animals or in
Man, is to accurately diagnose it early and undertake some control measures quickly. Hundreds of tumors are removed from animals every day, and few are sent into the lab for biopsy because
of owner concern over cost. My feeling is that if a tumor is worth
removing, it is worth sending to the lab for analysis. This information tells you what steps to take to control this serious disease.

Cancer is a scary word, and it alarms owners to hear that their
pet has cancer. However, with early detection and new treatments, many of these pets can live relatively normal lives.

Q: *The vet tells us our cat has some sort of cancer in its lymph
nodes. Now we are going to have to put the cat through
chemotherapy. Do you think it's worth trying?*

A: Only you can decide if the expense and trouble of intensive
therapy for your cat is worth it to you. With my pets, I would
spare no expense to help them. However, many people have
different levels of attachment to their pets. There can also be
other pragmatic considerations when considering the expense
of intensive treatment.

Your doctor sounds like he is very up-to-date on cancer treatments and could do the best for your cat. Lymphatic cancer, commonly a lymphoscarcoma, is the most common type of cancer in the cat. It is directly related to the incidence of feline leukemia virus (FeLV) in cats.

The use of chemotherapy has expanded quite a bit in the last decade. In humans, chemotherapy is often very aggressive with the goal of achieving a cure. In pets, the aim is less on a cure and more on getting an acceptable remission of the disease so the cat can live with a decent quality of life. Therefore, chemotherapy is not as serious or life threatening in cats as it is in humans.

Before you launch into chemotherapy for your cat, you will want to ask your veterinarian these questions: Is there a good likelihood of success, and is the cat in good enough health to withstand the therapy?

Ask yourself if you can and want to spend the money for intensive therapy and if you are prepared to deal with the possible side effects the therapy may bring on.

Q: *Our vet ran a FeLV test, and it came back positive. He said this meant our cat has leukemia. We are very afraid of losing him. What can we do?*

A: Although the two often go together, no veterinarian can say, based on a positive FeLV test alone, that a cat has leukemia! A positive test only means the cat has been exposed to FeLV.

The cat could fend the virus off and recover. It could become a carrier and never show signs of disease. There is only about a 30% chance that the cat will develop an FeLV-related disease, only one of which is leukemia.

If your cat does have leukemia, treatment of this form of blood cell cancer is not very successful. Before you become too upset about the leukemia diagnosis, I would seek a second opinion from another veterinarian. Have the FeLV test run again within a few months and see where the cat stands. Your cat may be healthy enough to fight it off.

Q: *My cat, Rhonda, has had smelly breath for months now. Because she is fourteen years old, I thought it was just bad teeth.*

The other day I looked in her mouth and was shocked to find an ugly growth. The vet says it's a squamous something-or-other. When she said it was cancer, I was shocked. What is that?

A: Squamous cell carcinoma, or SCC, is a very common type of cancer in cats. It primarily affects areas in the mouth. It is most common in older cats and can be quite bad if it has time to invade the gum, teeth and jaw bones.

If not diagnosed early, surgery is usually not successful because the tumors tend to invade into all of the different mouth structures. Because mouth tumors are invasive and may spread, they usually require aggressive treatment. Many veterinarians will use cryotherapy to freeze the tumor, if it has not spread too far.

If the tumor has spread into other surrounding structures, a combination of chemotherapy and radiation therapy seems to be the only other option. The outlook is not good for these cases.

Q: *Our cat has breast cancer. The vet did not give us a very good outlook. Should we have her breast removed?*

A: Breast cancer in both dogs and cats is not uncommon. It is primarily seen in older cats and cats that have not been spayed. In fact, it is seven to ten times more likely to occur in cats that have *not* been spayed. (Another very good reason to spay your cat!)

Many of these mammary tumors are malignant and difficult to control. They tend to grow rapidly and invade the underlying muscles of the abdomen. Some of them open to the outside and are pretty ugly.

The best treatment is mastectomy. If both chains of breast tissue are involved, both should be removed. This can be done at one time or in two different surgeries, depending on what your doctor decides is best. Chemotherapy has not proven to be very helpful in feline breast cancer, so removal of the breast is your best bet.

As to whether it is advisable, I cannot answer that for you. It depends on your attachment to your cat and your ability, both financially and emotionally, to endure the course of treatment. I can tell you that the average length of survival in cats treated for breast cancer with surgery is about a year.

Q: *We thought our cat had FUS for many months. Even though we'd done everything the vet told us to do, he still showed signs of the problem. Finally, the doctor took an X ray of the bladder and found a tumor. Is this common, and can it be cured?*

A: It is not common, but it does occur. You should be glad your veterinarian is so sharp. This is a condition that could have gone undiagnosed for many years—even forever.

The most common tumor of the cat's bladder is what is called a transitional cell carcinoma. There are some very unique cells that line the walls of the bladder and the urethra (urine tube). The cells that line the bladder are different from those that line the urethra. In order to change cell types from bladder to urethra, there are a series of transitional cells that make up the wall area near the part of the bladder that leads into the tube. These transitional cells are susceptible to cancer development and are the most common place for bladder tumors to develop.

The history and signs are exactly as you have described. The cat will appear as though it has a bladder infection, but it will not respond to antibiotics. The tumor is usually diagnosed by taking an X ray of the bladder and seeing the spot on the film. The only treatment for this problem is surgery. Because this type of tumor is very invasive, even excellent surgery may not get it all. Therefore the prognosis is not good for this type of cancer.

Q: *We have an eight-month-old kitty named Porche. He has an ulcer-type spot on his neck. The vet said he thought it was a "mass cell." He began talking about surgery. When we heard your show today we thought we'd get your opinion.*

A: Your veterinarian probably said "mast cell tumor." This is a relatively common type of skin cancer seen in cats under one year of age. It usually occurs on the lips, face and neck and appears to be lumps under the skin, although some may ulcerate.

Treatment is, in fact, surgery. The doctor may also take a local lymph node to check for spread of this cancer to other areas of the cat's body, which is quite common with mast cell cancer. About 25% to 50% of all mast cell tumors removed from cats recur after surgery. Some doctors will give the cat steroids to help shrink the tumor.

It is felt that some of these tumors regress on their own. I would not let my cat go without treatment if I knew he had a mast cell tumor, but no doubt some cats have them and recover from them without our ever knowing.

Q: *Our ten-year-old cat, Randy, was lame for several months before we took him in for a check. The doctor seemed quite concerned over the pain in Randy's leg. He took some X rays and said he suspects bone cancer! He has recommended surgery, which sounds very expensive. What would you do?*

A: If I were your veterinarian I would probably encourage you to take some more X rays and blood tests in order to see if we could accurately determine what is going on.

Bone cancer in cats is rare, but it does occur. Osteosarcoma is the type of bone cancer that accounts for about 70% of all bone cancer in cats. This is not good news because this is a very malignant type of bone cancer in which the prognosis is not good.

The treatment for this cancer is surgical amputation of the affected limb in order to prevent movement of the cancer to other parts of the body. Historically, cats may live several years after a surgery such as this.

Although I don't know the type of tumor involved, and there are many different types, I would recommend an aggressive approach. You cannot wait on cancer. It can spread quickly and make the outcome much more serious. If it does prove to be bone cancer, I would go with your veterinarian's recommendation.

CHAPTER 20

Heart and Respiratory Disease

"My wife feeds our cat all kinds of scraps from the table, mostly cheese and other fatty things. I told her the cat was going to have a heart attack and, sure enough, the cat had a heart attack! The vet said it was because of taurine in his diet."

The problem is actually a taurine deficiency in a cat's diet. This deficiency used to be quite common until the pet-food manufacturers began supplementing all cat foods with higher amounts of taurine.

This is a perfect example of the interesting interconnections between cats, environment and disease. Many people don't think of cats or dogs as having heart attacks, lung cancer or diabetes. Yet many cats succumb to these diseases every day and the astute veterinarian will properly diagnose and treat most of them.

In addition to complex heart disease, upper respiratory infections are very common in cats. In former times in veterinary medical history, sneezing cats were seen daily in animal clinics nationwide. Now, however, with the advent of modern vaccines against the major viral causes of respiratory disease, the number of sneezing cats seen in practice has dropped. Respiratory illnesses are still common, however, and can be serious.

Q: *Our Persian, Perry, has had trouble breathing and a poor appetite for the last few months. Our veterinarian said she would run some tests, but she found something on the physical examination that concerned her. She said Perry's heart was muffled and he did not have a good pulse in his rear legs. Our vet said it could be a problem with his heart. She named some long scientific term. Can you shed some light on this problem?*

193

A: She probably said your cat may have hypertrophic cardiomy-opathy. This is a serious disease of cats where the left ventricle of the heart becomes thickened. It seems especially prone to attack Persians. The breathing difficulty occurs because of fluid accumulation in the lungs, which by itself can be a seri-ous problem.

I do not want to scare you, but I have seen several of these cats die suddenly when a clot forms in their blood and causes a blockage of the brain, heart or other vital organs. Other cats may become weak or even paralyzed in the rear legs because the branching of the aorta to each rear leg causes a perfect place for these clots to lodge.

Your veterinarian is going to want to X-ray Perry's chest to see if the heart is enlarged. An echocardiograph machine, if available, is a very good diagnostic tool to determine exactly what is going on and how bad it is.

If Perry is suffering from hypertrophic cardiomyopathy, then you must handle him carefully. Too much vigorous han-dling can be life threatening in these cases. A variety of drugs can be given to prevent some serious secondary problems while trying to cure the primary problem.

The doctor will use Lasix, which is a diuretic to eliminate the lung fluid. Bronchodilators are also helpful. Believe it or not, some veterinarians are using nitroglycerin in severe cases. This drug helps stop some of the abnormal fluid load on the heart and is given as an ointment on the cat's ear. Two other drugs are very helpful in these cats. One is Cardizem and the other is Bayer children's aspirin.

Ask your doctor about the use of these drugs and what she feels is the long-term outlook for Perry. When treated properly and handled carefully, cats with this disease have lived over six years after diagnosis. Plan on keeping Perry indoors from now on and no vigorous kitty games.

Q: *Our vet says my cat has dilated cardiomyopathy. He didn't seem too concerned about his overall condition or future, but it sounded quite serious to me. I know it has to do with taurine deficiency, but can you fill me in with a few more details?*

A: This was a common disease in cats until it was discovered that most commercial cat foods were deficient in taurine. Now that most companies are supplementing with extra taurine, we see less and less of this problem. It primarily affects middle-aged cats of all breeds and sexes.

The signs seen are the same as for any problem affecting the heart muscle. These include weakness, breathing difficulty and paralysis in the rear legs. The doctor can diagnose the disease with X rays and an ECG (echocardiogram).

Clearly, the disease is treated by supplying adequate taurine in the cat's diet. However, when symptoms have already occurred, the cat will need intensive treatment for a while to correct these other problems. When the problem is caused by a taurine deficiency alone, the outlook is very good.

Your doctor will probably prescribe strict rest, diuretics, digoxin, vasodilators and aspirin. Even though your cat may now be on a good, taurine-fortified diet, most veterinarians recommend taurine supplementation until a month after the cat has stabilized.

Q: *My cat has sneezed for several weeks now. Nothing we treat him with seems to do the trick. Can you recommend some other medicine?*

A: Most sneezing in cats is caused by viral agents that bring about a typical syndrome of upper respiratory infection, or URI. Such viral infections are sometimes difficult to treat and can progress into severe infections with a lot of complications. Because there are no antiviral medications for this problem, we can only let the virus run its normal course of five to ten days and prevent secondary bacteria from taking over and causing infections by providing supportive care for the cat.

I like to use liquid antibiotics because cats suffering from URI usually have blocked nasal passageways and are likely to struggle during pilling. Amoxicillin liquid or Baytril work well because they are broad-spectrum antibiotics. Eye ointments are used to prevent secondary eye ulcers.

Keep the cat's nose and eyes clear of any discharge. I've used small amounts of Afrin, one drop per day, to help keep nasal congestion in check. Also, warm humidified air with Vicks vaporizer fluid helps.

All cats with URI should be kept warm! In severe cases, where the cat has stopped eating or drinking, I suggest forced nutrition with NutriCal and subcutaneous fluids. Remember, because these cats cannot smell, they will often stop eating. Also, these cats typically run a fever and may have sores in their mouths, which also contribute to a serious lack of appetite. Most often, when an upper respiratory infection becomes fatal, it is because of lack of nutrition.

Q: *We have a cat with a severe upper respiratory infection that we are treating here at home. I was wondering if this disease can be passed to me or my children?*

A: There is no scientific evidence that the two major causes of upper respiratory disease in cats (feline herpes virus and feline calicivirus) can infect humans. Luckily most viruses like these are very specific, infecting only one type of animal. It never hurts to use good hygiene practices, however. After treating the cat you should clean the area very well and wash your hands.

Q: *We have a small cattery full of beautiful Siamese cats. It seems like every litter we have gets upper respiratory disease. Nothing we've done so far has stopped it. Any helpful hints?*

A: Preventing upper respiratory infections in catteries, or even multicat households, is difficult unless you have proper isolation facilities. If litters of kittens are born and raised in the same area as adult cats who are carriers of these viruses, the kittens will be exposed to the virus at a very early age. They will develop the disease as soon as their maternal protection from mother's milk wears off, at about seven to eight weeks of age.

These kittens then become carriers of the virus, and the cycle of chronic upper respiratory infections continues. Carriers of the virus should first be identified and removed from your cattery. Pregnant cats should be isolated and stay isolated until their kittens have been vaccinated. Under normal circumstances, kittens should not be vaccinated until eight to nine weeks of age, otherwise the mother's immunity will neutralize the vaccine. Kittens in multicat settings, where exposure to chronic respiratory infections has been a problem, should be vaccinated following the program developed by the Cornell Feline Health Center.

- Administer intranasal vaccine at two weeks of age.
- Administer injectable vaccine at four weeks of age.
- Wean kittens by six weeks of age.
- Separate kittens from adult cats until four months of age.
- Administer injectable vaccine at eight weeks and fourteen weeks of age.
- When the kittens are sixteen weeks of age, they can join the rest of the group.

Q: *Our cat had a very bad bout with sneezing, drooling and not eating for two weeks. Our vet said he thought it was cal ci virus. Can you tell me what that is?*

A: It is calicivirus, and it is quite common. It can cause mild disease in one case and very severe disease in another. Signs include fever, loss of appetite, sneezing and ulcers in the mouth due to the virus replicating there. Oddly enough, some cats even get a weird strain that causes limping and arthritis, related to cartilage damage.

The virus is carried by apparently normal cats in their mouths. Calicivirus (FCV for feline calicivirus) is one of the upper respiratory pathogens that must run its course while we make sure the cat is protected against stress and secondary invaders. The cat can easily become a carrier for weeks, months or even life. I would strongly suggest you properly sanitize your premises if you have any other cats in the house. This virus can live for eight to ten days outside the body but is quite susceptible to antiviral disinfectants.

FCV is one of the diseases we vaccinate for, so be sure this cat and any others in the household are vaccinated.

Q: *We had a cat with pneumonitis last year and would like to know how to prevent it in our new kitten that has just arrived.*

A: Generally speaking, the time to think about prevention in a situation like this is *before* you bring a susceptible animal into the environment. However, if it has been some time since the infection in your other cat, you are probably all right.

Pneumonitis is caused by a chlamydia organism called *Chlamydia psittaci*. It is actually seen in less than 5% of all feline respiratory infections. Its major presenting signs are a pus discharge from the eyes, sneezing and a fever. This organism can be killed with medicated eye drops. A vaccine is now available for pneumonitis and is often included in annual vaccinations for cats with high exposure, show cats, breeding animals or those in catteries. Ask your veterinarian what he thinks your kitten's exposure risk is.

CHAPTER 21

Diseases Contagious to People

"Doc Jim, I think my daughter got a head full of ringworms from the cat. I can see 'em crawling all in her hair."

Q: *What does a ringworm look like?*

A: Actually, there is no such worm as a ringworm. The *condition* called ringworm is caused by a fungus, *not* a worm. This particular type of fungus is known as a dermatophyte and is very common. Although over fifty dermatophytes are known to affect man, only twelve have ever involved animals. Of these, only about four are common in people and of those, only one is very common. That one is *Microsporum canis* found only in dogs and cats.

This type of ringworm requires close contact to be transmitted. It is seen more frequently in children because of the way kids will carry a cat around their neck, or sleep with a dog curled up against their soft, easily infected skin.

Another common way people get ringworm from pets is by allowing an affected pet to sleep on clothes or pillowcases. By wearing these clothes or sleeping on the pillowcase, there is sufficient, close, prolonged contact to human skin to cause dermatophyte infection.

Q: *Our son got ringworm from our cat. We are treating Robby's spots and have put the cat outside at our physician's insistence, but she sure is lonely out there. Can't we treat the cat, too?*

A: You sure can! I can always tell a physician who is not an animal lover. They always banish the animal, rather than work with you to actually cure the problem. The answer to this problem is *not* putting the cat outside. The cat, if he is in fact the source of the infection, will simply get worse and even be exposed to more dirt, which is where many ringworm spores reside.

Bring kitty in and bathe her in an antifungal shampoo like Nolvasan shampoo. Ask your pet store operator or veterinarian to make a recommendation, but I'd look for tamed iodine or some specific reference to fungicidal action on the label. In reality, just a good bath will get rid of most of the problem. Then, if the cat is the source of the infection, you need to put her on the oral antifungal drug called Gresiofulvin. If there are any obvious spots of hair loss, treat those directly with an antifungal ointment, such as Tinactin. There is now a new vaccine that both treats and prevents ringworm. Ask your veterinarian about Fel-O-Vax MC-K.

Most cases of ringworm in cats can be cleared up within a week or two with good treatment. There are persistent cases that will take longer. Work with your veterinarian to clear up kitty and let your physician take care of Robby. I'll bet within a few weeks you'll have everybody back to normal.

By the way, some ringworm in animals is transmitted to them by humans, but I would never recommend you put Robby out.

Q: *My friend got ringworm and the doctor said it was tinea capitis. He said she should use a special shampoo, take some pills and get rid of the cat. Does she really need to get rid of the cat?*

A: NO, she needs to get rid of that doctor! Tinea capitis is caused by *Microsporum audouini*. Cats do not carry that particular fungus. Dogs and cats are responsible for *Microsporum canis* infections in people, and the two may look very similar, so I can understand some confusion. However, if the doctor knows it is tinea capitis he should know cats don't transmit that dermatophyte.

I would still bathe the cat and would recommend that her veterinarian look at the cat and perhaps run a test called dermatophyte test medium, or DTM This will tell if the cat is the culprit or if it is something else in your friend's environment.

As an example, tinea capitis can be transmitted fairly easily from direct skin to skin contact, especially from the backs of theater seats, barber clippers or contaminated clothing.

Q: *We were recently visiting in Florida and heard they were having a problem with rabies. They showed a cat that was caught on the side of a road and was tested positive for rabies. That was pretty scary. I thought rabies was mostly a dog problem.*

A: Many people think that, and consequently, we have a large population of cats out there that are not vaccinated for rabies. This does make them more susceptible as a whole and therefore a serious risk to humans.

In the past decade we have seen a rise in rabies in cats. Because many cats may not show typical signs of rabies once infected, they could potentially expose many people to this deadly disease. Therefore the best way to set your mind at ease is to keep your cats vaccinated.

Believe it or not, in some areas where rabies is a serious threat every year, people vaccinate their horses for rabies.

Q: *My mother is allergic to cats. She loves to come visit us but she has to take antihistamines and is miserable most of the time. Would it help to banish the cats outside?*

A: Banishing the cats outside won't help, because the dander which your mother is allergic to, while produced by the cats, is everywhere in your house and that is the source of most of the offending material.

It is currently estimated that between 25% and 30% of the population is sensitive to their pets. This means that sixty to seventy-five million Americans are adversely affected when exposed to pets. Cats are by far the most allergenic pet, but any animal with fur or feathers can cause a human allergic reaction.

Symptoms range from itchy, watery eyes, watery nasal discharge, congestion, coughing, wheezing, difficulty breathing and itchy skin or hives.

Oddly enough it's not the pet's hair that causes the allergic reaction, but what's under it—the dander. Dander is simply dead skin which is constantly shed into the environment. If a pet has been in the house for a long time, its dander will have permeated the entire house. It's not uncommon for an allergy sufferer to have symptoms for months after the pet has been removed from the house.

There are now sprays for pets that will help keep these dander flakes from coming off and seeding the home with allergen. Check out Allerpet made by Farnam. It was developed after years of research, and people are reporting very good results.

Q: Is it true that the Rex cat is less allergenic that others?
A: No that is *not* true. Many people believe this because the Rex has very short hair. In fact there are even shorter-haired cats, even hairless ones, that can still cause allergic reactions because it is not the hair, but the dander which causes the problem. It's the skin's normal and natural turnover that causes the dander to form, and it's the dander that's the culprit.

Knowing that it is the dander that causes the problem, you then understand that it makes no difference if your pet is long-haired or shorthaired, sheds excessively or hardly at all.

In addition to the dander, cat's saliva contains a potent bacterial protein allergen. Because cats are such methodical self-groomers and spend 30% to 50% of their day licking their fur, they spread these allergens over their bodies when they preen. The saliva dries on the hair and eventually flakes off and becomes airborne. This allergen is the smallest of all known allergens and penetrates deep into lung tissue.

I know this all sounds like bad news for those of you who are allergic to cats. However, in the past few years there have been several products developed to help cleanse the hair of these allergens and therefore control their dispersal into the environment.

They also condition the skin and hair, which reduces future accumulations of both dander and saliva on the hair. Many allergic cat lovers have known for years to simply rinse their cat in distilled water every week. This keeps these dander and saliva materials off the hair coat and drastically decreases the owner's allergy symptoms.

Q: *I've just become pregnant and my doctor asked if I owned a cat. When I told him we had two, he warned us about toxoplasmosis. He sounded a little serious when he spoke of this and really cautioned me to stay away from their litter box. Can you give us more details?*

A: You bet. Toxoplasmosis is a serious disease. If one acquires this disease during pregnancy it can cause birth defects, abortion or stillbirths. It is caused by a relatively common parasite organism called *Toxoplasma gondii*. Most people who get toxoplasmosis have very few symptoms. Therefore, you could be infected with the disease and not know it. In fact about 30% of Americans are exposed during their lifetime.

Toxoplasma comes from the only animal known to shed the parasite in its feces, the common household cat. If your cat is infected, you can get the parasite in your system from its litter box or from the garden. Emphasis is placed on prevention rather than treatment. Veterinarians do not routinely screen cats for the parasite, as the value of this test is questionable.

Removing your cat from the household during pregnancy is of little value, as the parasite can remain in the soil around your house for eighteen months. Therefore the key to this problem is prevention.

Here are the key points:
- Confine your cats inside to prevent hunting as they can become infected by eating killed birds and rodents.
- Feed your cats only commercially prepared diets. Do not feed raw meats of any kind.
- The litter box should be cleaned daily. As an expectant mother, let someone else do this chore. Do not spread the litter in the yard or garden.
- Use the new clumping type cat litters, as they are more sanitary and keep the box cleaner.
- Eat only thoroughly cooked meat. Cook pork or lamb especially well.
- Wash your hands thoroughly after handling meat, vegetables and cats.
- Wear gloves while gardening, and wash your hands well when finished.

- Prevent cats from defecating in a child's sandbox by keeping it covered when not in use.
- Do not drink raw milk, especially goat's milk.

As you can see, common personal hygiene procedures will prevent most potential exposures to toxoplasmosis.

Q: *I had no idea children could get roundworms from pets. What can we do to prevent that?*

A: It is not a major concern, but it does occur. Most cases are a result of children eating dirt. This is a common behavior in children and results in many cases of ascariasis every year. Roundworm in children is mostly seen in tropical countries where both environmental and sanitation conditions lend themselves to this disease. As many as half of the kids in those countries have roundworms. Ascariasis in this country is primarily limited to the Southeast.

The problem with ascariasis in people is with the migration of the parasite larvae through the child's lungs. Symptoms include cough, wheezing and fever. Heavy infestations may make nutritional deficiency worse. Aside from the larval migration, the adult worms can cause their share of damage as well.

This can be prevented with good sanitation and teaching your children to wash their hands after playing outside in the dirt and with pets.

Take your cats to your veterinarian and have them tested for roundworms. If they are worm free, you have one less source to worry about. However, remember that stray cats can come into your back yard and spread the parasite in your yard, sandbox and garden, so hand washing is important.

Q: *We saw a report on a morning news show about cat scratch disease. We didn't really understand it, but the doctor on the report was quite serious about it. What is cat scratch disease?*

A: I'm glad you asked. Cat scratch disease is nothing more than a bacterial infection at the site of a bite or scratch. The bacteria suspected is Pasteurella, but scientists have yet to confirm this. Children seem to be mostly affected because kids play more roughly with cats and their skin is more easily scratched.

The disease is actually inflammation of the local lymph nodes near the scratch or bite. This can be seen from a few days to two weeks after the scratch. There is really nothing special about this disease except it is the source of a few sensationalistic news reports every year. If a doctor suspects this disease he simply places the patient on antibiotics and it is over in a week or two.

Cats really got a bad rap on this one. The same syndrome has been seen with dog scratches and bites and even monkey scratches. If you or your children are scratched by the family cat, as will inevitably happen, simply clean the scratch with antibacterial soap. If redness persists longer than a few days, and if a lymph node becomes swollen and sore, you may want to see your doctor for a course of antibiotics.

Q: *We picked up a little stray cat last week. Among other things he has sarcoptic mange. The vet is treating our kitty with warm soapy water bathes and a lime–sulfur solution. He said if any of us start scratching, we should see our doctor. How contagious is this? We're concerned.*

A: Feline scabies, or sarcoptic mange, is caused by a little mite called *Notoedres cati*. Although it is not the same mite that causes scabies in humans or dogs, it is highly contagious. If you have any other cats in the house, they will have to be treated with the same lime–sulfur dips. If not, don't be too concerned about human transmission. Although possible, if you take good precautions, it is not likely.

After you handle the cat, for treatment or petting, wash your hands well. I'd recommend using gloves for the treatment because you will be stirring up the skin flakes and scales where there is a high concentration of mites.

If anyone in your family begins to itch, your doctor will prescribe simple treatments. In people, this mite is self-limiting, which means they cannot reproduce, but they can cause itching and redness for a time.

Your cat will most likely be mite free in three weeks, so hang in there and use common sense about how you and your family handle the kitty. Bless you for taking care of her.

CHAPTER 22

Stomach, Intestinal and Kidney Problems

"Doc, this afternoon our cat came in from the garage with something in its mouth. My son said it was fishing line! Sure enough, it is 20# test line. When I pulled on it, it did not give and the cat seems to be in pain. I investigated the garage and found that we had left some catfish bait on our hooks from a fishing trip last weekend. You don't suppose our cat has swallowed hook, line and sinker, do you?"

I've treated four such cases in my years of practice. They all required surgery to remove the hook and a few carefully placed incisions in the stomach and intestinal tract to remove the line.

Curiosity can indeed kill the cat! It has killed many of them. Normally, cats are very careful about what they eat. However, many ingest foreign objects that can cause serious injury or death.

Cats have more than their fair share of kidney disease. Chronic renal disease affects many cats and sadly, it causes many cats to be put to sleep. Although we can help these cats somewhat with treatment, it is best to prevent renal disease with the highest quality nutrition possible.

Q: *Our beautiful Maine Coon Cat, Jenny, has been diagnosed with kidney disease. The vet has sent us home with lots of medicine and samples of new cat food. What caused this?*

A: Chronic renal failure is a very slow onset, irreversible deterioration of the kidneys that results in decreased kidney function.

It is caused by various things: exposure to toxic chemicals, cancer, infections, injuries, and it can even be hereditary. The problem with this disease is that by the time it is diagnosed, about 75% of the functional capabilities of both kidneys are gone. Unfortunately, it is at this point that the remaining kidney function can't keep up with the cat's body demands for maintaining normal body fluid levels and excreting normal metabolic toxins.

The aim of treatment is to use fluid therapy to correct the dehydration that is usually present. In addition, we try to correct metabolic imbalances that occur when the kidneys cannot control the chemical balance of removing waste products from the body.

If the kidneys have not failed, but are doing their best to keep up their job, preventive nutrition can help the cat live many years. Ask your veterinarian about nutritional support along with his recommended medical treatment.

Q: *When our cat was diagnosed with renal failure we were devastated, but he has responded well to treatment. Now, six months later, he is going downhill again. The doctor has suggested diuresis. Is that going to help? Is it worthwhile?*

A: The object of diuresis is to maintain good blood flow to the kidneys and enhance the normal flow of urine so the cat's body can rid itself of the normal waste chemicals that are generated through metabolism.

There are different types of diuresis used in cats. The type your doctor uses depends on the severity of the disease, how the cat has responded to treatment thus far, his urine output, any complicating conditions and your time and commitment to this process.

The doctor may just use fluids for this process, or he can use fluids plus diuretic drugs. The first few days or even weeks, this will be done in the hospital. Then you can take him home for a low-stress environment and nutritional support. At regular checkups, if the cat needs further diuresis, the doctor and staff will arrange a schedule for you.

Nutrition is a very important part of the after care of this kind of treatment. Cats love high fat and high protein foods. They will usually eat better at home where there is less stress and when they are feeling better after the diuresis has helped them over the initial crisis. Try different types of foods, warm it or try adding some warm chicken broth or clam juice to get kitty interested. The best thing to do is feed a diet commercially prepared just for this problem, but many cats refuse it. Tempt him the best you can. If all else fails, you can make a homemade diet for him. Your veterinarian can give you a few recipes. Good luck!

Q: *Yesterday, about an hour after we used some flea powder on our cat, he threw up. Do you think the powder made him sick?*

A: It is possible, but more likely it is a condition called esophagitis. Cats spend most of their day preening or grooming themselves. Therefore, anything you put on a cat ends up in its mouth, down its esophagus and in its stomach. Flea powders are pretty irritative, besides their chemical toxic nature. Therefore, my guess is that your cat got a pretty good dose of this powder in its mouth and esophagus and the result was an inflammation of the esophagus.

This is a minor and short-lived inflammation and will usually go away by itself. For this reason, I usually do not recommend the use of powders on cats. I like to use a flea spray, rubbed into the fur and then give the cat a quick wipe with a towel to remove any excess chemical on the surface of the fur.

You might look for a new device called a Brush-ette. It is a brush that delivers flea chemical down to the surface of the skin (where the fleas are) with less of the chemical on the surface of the fur to be licked up by the cat. You can find it at your neighborhood pet store.

Q: *We bought a new cat food yesterday, and our cats seemed to like it a lot. However, this morning I noticed a little ropelike shape of cat-food-colored stuff on the floor. Why did someone throw up their food?*

A: Both dogs and cats have a very important and sensitive protective mechanism—vomiting! When their little stomachs sense that something is new, different, spicy, too high in this, or too low in that, they'll throw it up. This is good because it keeps many cats alive after eating something that would hurt them if left to go through the gastrointestinal tract. However, it also causes what you've just described.

A change in diet is one reason cats will regurgitate food. They may also do this when they eat too much, too fast. This is especially annoying when it is pet food colored and it is left on your white carpet or sofa.

There is probably no medical problem here, unless it continues to occur.

Q: *Our cat was vomiting regularly for about a week when we took him to the vet. After many tests and X rays, the vet decided to operate. She removed twelve rubber bands from our cat's stomach! Why would he eat rubber bands?*

A: Why do cats do most of what they do? My cats have always seemed interested in rubber bands. The smell or the texture of the rubber must be appealing to them. I've removed rubber balls, rubber toys and rubber bands from pet's stomachs, and there is always a severe gastritis associated with the foreign object in contact with the stomach wall for some time.

Try to kitty proof your house and pick up all rubber bands, otherwise your kitty will do it again.

Q: *Last Christmas Eve our cat became very sick. When we took him to the emergency clinic they ran various tests. They decided to operate and found he had a punctured intestine in seven places because of tinsel from the tree! Have you ever heard of that?*

A: Oh yes! In fact, I've spent two Christmas Eves doing just that. Once in a cat and once in a Dachshund. What happens is the long, stringlike nature of the tinsel will get caught in the normal twisted intestinal track. Then it doesn't go anywhere. The intestine tries its best to remove this by moving up and down over this stuck piece of string or tinsel. This creates a sawing action and everywhere the tinsel is on the inside of a bend of intestine, it will cut through, over time. This creates multiple intestinal perforations and a very acute crisis. These pets will die within hours if not diagnosed and treated quickly.

I recommend people with cats refrain from putting tinsel on Christmas trees, or at least on the bottom one third.

Q: *Our cat, Frannie, has been vomiting off and on for about a month. Sometimes there is blood in it. She has lost weight and now has diarrhea. What do you think she has?*

A: Symptoms such as these can indicate any number of diseases. It is impossible for me to diagnose such a thing over the radio because of the endless possibilities. However, there is a condition called inflammatory bowel disease that shows the signs you describe. Laboratory tests are usually within normal limits, and the only way to diagnose this particular disease is with an intestinal biopsy.

Now obviously you would not undertake such a procedure without going through basic tests and ruling out the obvious things that can cause the same symptoms. But I have seen many cases of this condition, and your veterinarian may have to test for it. It is important, in the long term, to rule out this disease because its treatment is specific.

To treat inflammatory bowel disease, we use steroids to stop the inflammation, antibiotics to decrease the likelihood of secondary bacterial infection and sometimes hypoallergenic food. Work with your veterinarian toward diagnosing the exact cause first, then treat specifically for what the doctor finds.

Q: *Our cat has diarrhea. Can we treat that at home?*

A: Probably not. Diarrhea in cats is caused by many things. Sure, an upset stomach from different food, spoiled food or too big a mouse will cause a transient diarrhea that will go away shortly or with some home treatment. However, diarrhea can also be caused by parasites or worms that cannot be treated at home. Foreign bodies like hair balls, small toys, cloth or any number of things can also cause this problem and treatment at home would only delay proper treatment and cause a potentially critical time delay that could be costly. Bacterial and viral infections are also another major cause of diarrhea in cats. Even protozoa can cause diarrhea in cats.

If you attempt to treat diarrhea in cats at home, you run the risk that the cat has one of these more serious causes but the diarrhea responds temporarily because of the treatment. Then, later, the cat may lapse back into more severe signs. I'd like to see you get the little guy to a veterinarian immediately. If it is something simple, the diagnosis and treatment will be quick and inexpensive. If it is not something simple, you need to know that NOW!

Q: *Our cat, Julie, has been vomiting off and on for the past six months. First it was monthly, then weekly, now it appears she vomits up her food about every other day. Our vet has run every test in the book. After listening to your show we even put her on a hypoallergenic diet with no change. What else can we do?*

A: There is a syndrome that is not that uncommon called idiopathic vomiting syndrome. This occurs in cats with a history just as you have described. The cat vomits with increasing frequency, and all tests are normal. It usually vomits up food, but is not depressed or losing weight at all.

You may want to ask your veterinarian about using the dog birth-control pill called Ovaban on Julie. This is a powerful antivomiting drug and has been used quite successfully with these cases in a decreasing-dosage regime. Good luck.

CHAPTER 23

Injuries,
Environmental Stress
and Poisonings

"Is it true that a cat can fall from several stories, land on its feet and walk away without an injury?"

"Cats do land on their feet from a fall, but I wouldn't count on it not having injuries."

"And they can do that nine times, right?"

Cats actually seem to suffer frequent injuries because of their innate curiosity and because they are agile and able to get into many dangerous situations. They are fragile and their skin is thin, making them susceptible to injuries and dangerous situations.

On the other side of the coin, cats heal well. We used to remark in practice that cats make us look good after repairing a wound or injury because of the uncanny way cats heal.

This is not to say that feline injuries are not serious and some of the things that happen to cats are unbelievable. As the operator of a large metropolitan veterinary emergency hospital for several years, I would think I'd just about seen it all, until the next case came in.

Q: Why do you feel so strongly that cats should be kept indoors?

A: Did you know that cats who live outdoors live an average of one year? Cats who live indoors live an a average of thirteen years! That's a dramatic difference.

Cats who go outdoors are exposed to other cats that can

carry disease or cause fights. They are susceptible to attacks by dogs and wild animals. They may get hit by a vehicle, get into some poison or toxic chemical or even be shot at by mischievous kids.

Indoor cats who go outdoors only occasionally may be at even greater risk because they are less streetwise. As the director of a large emergency animal clinic for several years, I saw just about every kind of emergency you could imagine, and most could have been prevented by keeping cats indoors.

Q: *I agree with you that cats should be inside pets, but ours will not urinate in his litter box—we've tried everything. So now it's either he goes outside or to the shelter. How can we make it safe for him outside?*

A: If you must let your cat outdoors, either because of living arrangements or house soiling problems, at least have a safe place for the cat to escape to. Installing a kitty door into a garage or porch will allow a place for the cat to seek safe haven in case of attack.

Kitty-proof your garage and back yard. Put toxic chemicals out of reach, put sharp objects away and look at everything with a critical eye. Make sure he has a litter box in the garage, and you may even want to feed him there so that he knows he can find safety and security in there.

I have seen special fences built around back yards to keep cats in. You may want to look into that and see if the time and expense is something you can do.

A cattery is something you may want to investigate. You can attach it to your house or your garage with a kitty door. These can be any size, fully enclosed screened areas that allow the cat to be outside, but fully protected from animals and other threats.

Q: *The other morning I was surprised when I started my car and heard a loud thump and yowl. I looked just in time to see a neighborhood cat running with a limp away from the car. I could not find it to help. Why do cats get up into car motors?*

A: Cats look for a warm, cozy place to sleep during cold months.

They will crawl up inside the engine compartment of a car and sleep there because the car motor will stay warm for many hours after it's turned off.

Wary owners will learn to open the hood and look underneath for sleeping cats before starting cars. At least bang on the hood to wake them up before starting the engine. This is a common injury in the winter, and cats can come out with anything from minor scrapes to fatal wounds. It depends on how quickly they get out and what route they take! The fan blades and belts are the most dangerous and often take at least one good swipe at the unsuspecting kitty.

Q: *Our cat is always coming in with cuts and small bite wounds. Can you give us the proper way to treat these things at home, using some first aid techniques?*

A: Much of first aid is common sense. With cuts, scrapes and bite wounds, the idea is to treat them quickly to prevent serious infection, the leading complication with these wounds.

First, I recommend you clip the hair away from the wound. Next, carefully wash the wound with a mild soap or an iodine-based soap, like Betadine. Rinse the cut and gently dry it. Use a cotton swab and clean the area with hydrogen peroxide. Bite wounds are usually deep punctures and may seal up on the surface without your even knowing there is an injury. If you see an obvious bite wound, clip the hair away, look for other wounds and clean the area as I've said, but don't use hydrogen peroxide. It can get down into tracts that lead under the skin, and the explosive expansion of free oxygen within the layers of skin can be damaging and painful.

If an area becomes hot, red, swollen and oozing, days, or even weeks, after a fight, this is an abscess and can really make your cat sick. I recommend you clip the hair, clean the surface and look for other areas where the skin is soft, friable and ready to break open. Carefully hot pack the area with a face cloth, using hot tap water, for twenty-minute sessions to help the microcirculation and speed healing.

Many of these injuries must be seen by a doctor, so I'd suggest letting your veterinarian take a look. Bad cases will need minor surgery, antibiotics and lots of good nursing care for a week or two.

Q: *Our inquisitive little cat got stung by a wasp today. We decided to treat it with baking soda instead of taking him to the vet. What else can we do?*

A: Good job! For insect stings I suggest you clean the area with hydrogen peroxide and use cold packs to prevent the venom from spreading. A compress of baking soda may help—just as it does with people, but that is assuming the cat is going to stay still and let you hold this stuff in place!

Many minor stings go away on their own within a few hours or days. However, some cats may develop severe reactions, even fatal ones. If your cat is having difficulty breathing, is convulsing or seems to be in severe pain, call the doctor and get the little guy to the emergency room.

Q: *Our cat came in limping this morning after having been gone a few days. Should we give him something or just take him to the vet?*

A: If your cat is limping, any number of problems might exist. Sting, fight wound, abscess, fracture, tendon rupture or cut are all possibilities. I recommend you confine the cat to a small area like a shipping kennel. If the leg is swollen, hot packs are good for relieving pain.

If it is obvious that the leg is broken, you can immobilize the leg using a rolled-up magazine that is taped around the leg. This is only temporary, of course, and helps you get to the doctor's office with minimal secondary damage.

Be careful about giving your cat any medicine out of your medicine cabinet. You may have aspirin and tranquilizers at home and, while these things may be used eventually, resist giving them to your cat as a first aid measure. Dosages vary, your veterinarian may need to give something at the clinic that would be complicated by premedication, and so on. Your best bet is to get the cat to the hospital as soon as practical.

Q: *Our cat got into a fight last night, and this morning we've noticed his left ear is torn right down the middle of the flap. What should we do?*

A: I would get him to your veterinarian today. He can suture up the ear and gain a pretty good cosmetic effect if the surgery is done early. The biggest enemy you have right now is time. The longer this type of wound is allowed to go on, the less likely it will heal without complications, including a poor cosmetic effect.

Cats heal very well. If the doctor can control the infection and the tissues are not damaged too badly, the ear will look fine. It will never look totally normal, but kitty will have a war wound to tell his buddies about.

By the way, while you're at the veterinarians, if your little guy is not neutered, speak with the doctor about doing that at the same time. One anesthetic will accomplish both things and will decrease the likelihood your cat will get into territorial fights again. You should also think about turning your cat into an indoor pet from now on. Outdoor cats succumb to much higher rates of injury and death.

Q: *We put a flea collar on our eight-year-old tabby yesterday and today he appears kind of slow or dizzy or something. Should we take it off?*

A: Yes, I've recommended for years people let a flea collar sort of "air out" for one to two days before putting them on pets. It seems the sudden release of the strong chemical will make some pets sick. Most often it is just as you have described. Cats, especially, will act sick and be lazy or dizzy. The symptoms are typically bad enough to be noticed. By simply removing the collar for a few days, the cat will bounce back and you can replace it with no further problems.

If, in your battle against fleas, you are using chemicals in the pet's environment and on the pet as well, some of this can be cumulative and cause the cat to be even more susceptible to overdose toxicity. Be careful in your applications. It is for this reason I have never recommended on-pet applications of concentrated chemicals, especially in cats. The package labels usually warn you not to use other chemicals while using these concentrates. This limits flea control to on the pet only, and this is most dangerous to your cat. So stick with the four-step approach outlined in Chapter 14.

Q: *We took our Persian, Fluff, to the groomers for a shampoo and dip. They called us later that day and said the cat was at the veterinary hospital because of a reaction to the dip. What gives?*

A: Persians are known for their hypersensitivity to flea chemicals. We never dip Persians because of this. Bathing with flea shampoos that are designed for cats, and the occasional use of flea sprays, will usually do the job. With Persians, you definitely must concentrate your flea control measures on the environment, not on the pet.

   With proper medical treatment your cat should recover just fine. Just know that she is sensitive to flea chemicals and take care in future applications.

Q: *There is some pus-like material in my cat's eye. I don't know if it is an injury or an infection. What can I do?*

A: Injuries to a cat's eyes are common. The best thing you can do for this is to clean any debris or pus from the eye using a home-made saline solution and a syringe.

   First, mix a half-teaspoon of salt with a cup of warm water. Then restrain the cat and, using your thumb and forefinger to spread the eyelids, quickly examine the eye.

   Using a syringe (if one is not available, use a basting syringe or eye dropper), hold the eyelids open and quickly flush the mixture across the eye.

   I guarantee the cat will resist. If you've been mostly successful in the flushing, don't continue to struggle, just let him go so he can get into a corner and calm down. You can repeat it later if need be.

   If you have a general ophthalmic ointment, you may use that to protect the eye until you can get the cat to a doctor. Just be careful that the ointment you use doesn't have steroids in it. While therapeutic for many conditions, steroids can actually make some injuries worse.

   Apply a small amount of ointment directly on the cornea, let the eyelids go back to their normal position and massage them a bit to spread the ointment around the cornea. It will also help to keep bright light away from your cat to ease its discomfort. If the swelling or redness persists, I would let your veterinarian take a look. The eye is not a structure you want to ignore.

Q: *Our fourteen-year-old cat was sleeping in the garage today and must have gotten too hot. He seems confused, is panting and is very hot. What can we do for him?*

A: Cats do not tolerate heat very well. If a cat has been exposed to heat and has not been able to cool its body, you will see the cat become dizzy, his breathing will be labored and rapid, his mouth will remain open, eyes glazed and he may even be unconscious.

The most important thing you can do is to cool him down. Wrap the cat in towels soaked in ice water, or you can wet his fur directly with alcohol. Alcohol evaporates very fast and cools the body quickly.

This should be done while someone is calling the emergency room and bringing the car around. Heat stroke is a severe emergency and must be handled immediately. Especially because he is old, this stress may be very hard on him, so please call your doctor right now and get him to the hospital.

Q: *We didn't realize it, but we left our old cat outside while we went into town. It was about 28°, and he was out for four hours. We found him by the garage door, and he is out of it. What can we do?*

A: Slowly rewarm his body, using warm, moist heat. I suggest you use towels soaked in hot tap water, no hotter than you can handle with your hands. Then simply wrap the cat or the body parts that appear to be affected. You will want to change the towels about every fifteen to twenty minutes.

Do not rub body parts you suspect may have frostbite, like ear tips, tail and paws. This can damage the skin further. Just use a warm-water towel pack, and get the cat to a veterinarian.

Q: *Our cat walked through some antifreeze yesterday, but it didn't appear to cause it any problem. However, today she is acting sick. Should we get her to a vet?*

A: Poisoning, especially antifreeze poisoning, is a common occurrence in outdoor cats. Antifreeze tastes and smells sweet, attracting cats and dogs as well as children. It takes only six milliliters of antifreeze to kill the average cat. They can get enough on their paws by walking through a spilled puddle in the garage to make them very sick.

Antifreeze can cause kidney damage in a matter of hours and can be fatal overnight. If you suspect your cat has consumed some antifreeze, there is no first aid you can do at home. Get him to the doctor immediately. Time is of the essence here as treatment is successful only if started as soon as possible.

To prevent this serious poisoning, keep antifreeze and other poisons up and out of the reach of pets and kids. Never store toxins in glass bottles. If you flush out your radiator and use new antifreeze, be sure to clean up very well and safely dispose of old radiator water.

PART VII

STRANGE, FUNNY,
WEIRD

CHAPTER 24

Full-Moon Saturdays!

It never fails. When Saturday rolls around and it's time to do my talk show, I always check to see if it's anywhere near a full moon. If so, I can be prepared for some very strange calls.

I remember when I was a boy, working with Dr. Baker, the rural veterinarian in Edinburg, Texas. He would be prepared for horses to bleed more profusely during and after surgery near periods of a full moon. Many farmers and ranchers would not let him schedule surgeries two to three days either side of a full moon!

I've spoken with emergency room physicians and nurses, police officers and others who are in a position to notice human behavior change, and they all agree: *weird things happen when the moon is full.*

I ran a busy animal emergency hospital in San Antonio, Texas, for two years. The staff and I came on duty at 6 PM and were through at 8 AM. It was a grueling schedule, but the work was *very* rewarding.

I can say, with some authority, that *both* human and animal behavior is different during a full moon. So it comes as no surprise to me that people who call my show when the moon is full, come up with some of the most interesting, entertaining and just plain weird calls I've ever received. I've told many of them they would end up in this book, so they have been forewarned. The names have been changed to protect the innocent.

There are some good pet care and training tips in this chapter, but you'll probably just enjoy reading some of the more unusual calls I get on national talk radio on full-moon Saturdays.

Why Do Cats Lick the Air?

"Our cats are pretty normal in every way except one. They lick the air! We have noticed this since they were little kitties. They will be sitting anywhere in the house, perfectly content and will begin licking the air. Why do they do that?"

I have heard of both dogs and cats doing this behavior. It appears to be a sensory intake of some kind. Kittens will learn that by "licking the air" they can take in some sensory information and later in life it can become a habit.

Both dogs and cats have vermosal glands on the inside of their mouths. These glands are like scent glands, and that is why many times you will notice that a very intent dog or cat will mouth breath. This allows them to take in every bit of sensory input they can get.

Don't worry about your kitties, they are probably quite normal.

Cat Watches TV

"Our cat watches TV. He loves it! He will sit and watch for hours. He sleeps on the TV, I guess because it is warm. It is especially funny when a bird or insect is on TV and he will go after it. It really upsets him when he can't get it.

We've noticed lately that he gets real upset with us when we come in the room and change the channel. The change upsets him, but we haven't noticed any particular program he likes more than another—except he does like your show!"

(Now if I could just get cats listening to my talk radio show, I could skip the middleman.)

Cat Thinks It's a Raccoon

"Dr. Jim, our cat does something weird. When he wants attention, he will walk over to us and stomp on our feet.

Typically, he'll use his back feet and just stomp on our feet until we pet him. Why does he do that?"

To get your attention—and it works quite well!

CATS AND SPAGHETTI

"I feed my cat spaghetti. He loves it. He has eaten it with all kinds of different sauces on it, but he mostly likes it plain or with a little butter on it. Is this OK for him?"

I always find it curious when someone tells me things they have done with their pet for years, then asks me if it's OK. Obviously many of these things are "OK" but probably not best for the pet's long-term health and well being. I must admit, however, spaghetti for cats is a new one on me!

MALE CAT WITH BREAST CANCER

"We just came home from the vet and are shocked. He said our very male cat, Tommy, has breast cancer. He is a very well-respected veterinarian, and we've been going there for some time, however, we were pretty skeptical when he said this. We have never heard of a man having breast cancer. How is it that male cats can?"

As it turns out, it can happen, although it is very rare. Both neutered and nonneutered male cats can develop carcinomas of the breast tissue, which is a normal part of their anatomy. The treatment is the same as if Tommy were a female, a mastectomy. Just don't tell the other cats on the block!

CAT LOVES TOFU

"As a part of a food hypersensitivity test, our veterinarian put our cat on tofu mixed with rice or potatoes. At first, JaLin resisted, but later took to the new kitty food. It seemed to help

her skin problem, and she was actually looking forward to her tofu and rice twice a day, but then it happened. The vet thought we should try her back on a few commercial pet foods. Dr. Jim, she just sits and yowls at the new food. She won't have anything but the tofu and rice."

I guess you'll just have to use a little kitty trickery and slowly mix the commercial food in with her tofu until you can get her eating the new diet. Try about 10% per day for ten days. It would be better for her because tofu and rice, while a good test diet, is not balanced for long-term health.

"Oh that's a great idea, we'll start weaning her over today!"

By the way, JaLin wouldn't be a Siamese Cat, would she?

"Yes, how did you know?"

Just a guess. . . .

CAT PURRS LIKE A TRACTOR

Let's go to Mobile, Alabama now and speak with George. . . .

"Dr. Jim, why do cats purr?"

Well, I believe there's no mystery to it. It is simply the air moving in and out of the cat's lungs passing by relaxed laryngeal folds (or vocal cords). When the cat is not relaxed these folds are pulled up and out of the air flow and they make no sound. When the cat is content, the folds are in the air flow and allowed to vibrate, making the happy sound.

"Well that's all very interesting, but I'll bet you didn't know that the frequency of a cat's purr is twenty-six cycles per second!"

Why, no, I did not know that!

"Yeah, and that just happens to be the same frequency as an idling diesel engine, too!"

Don't have enough to do in Mobile, George?

CAT DETECTS EARTHQUAKES

"Dr. Jim, we live in Palm Desert, California. As you may know, we get quite a few tremors running though the ground out here. I can always tell we are about to have a tremor because our cat, Malibu, will begin to act funny and run over to his food dish. Then a few minutes later we can feel it."

Well, that's interesting. I have heard of this before, but I believe this is the first cat that gets hungry when he feels an earthquake coming on. Maybe you can begin to correlate how much he eats with the magnitude of the quake!

CATS WALK LIKE GIRAFFES

"I read somewhere that cats walk like giraffes!" the caller announced proudly.

What do you mean by that?

"They pick up and set down the feet on one side of their body first, then the other side—just like a giraffe."

OK. I've never thought of this, but if you say it's true I'll buy that. . . . "Have you got a question for me today?" I said hopefully.

"Yeah, is that why they can walk along the top of a door frame and not fall off?"

MACHO CAT OWNER

A man called my show quite proud. He announced that his cat had been diagnosed with a case of stud tail.

(This is a secondary bacterial infection of an area of oil producing glands at the middle of a cat's tail. It is most commonly seen in intact male cats, and we often recommend neutering as a part of the treatment.)

> *"Yeah, the Doc wanted to neuter him. I told him 'No Way!'*
> *He's got a manly disease, he can get over it like a man.*
> *Besides no cat of mine is going to be an it!"*

Clearly the guy did not have a question for me, he just wanted to brag.

Index